Praise for *Don't Leave Your Friends Behind*

"These self-identified 'radical mothers' ‗
ture of self-help and literature, putting 'family values' in a new light and
on the agenda of social justice movements. And it's not just self-help for
radicals who are parents but food for everyone who seeks to become
their better, more compassionate selves."
—Roxanne Dunbar-Ortiz, activist, author, teacher

"This book is mind-blowing, brilliant, and urgently needed! It is full of
useful models and strategies for creating resistance that breaks down
barriers to participation for children and people caring for children, and
integrates deeply transformative commitments to building radically different activist culture and practice. This is a must-read for anyone trying
to build projects based in collective action."
—Dean Spade, author of *Normal Life: Administrative Violence, Critical
Trans Politics, and the Limits of Law*

"Here is required reading of the utmost importance: essays that will
help us all to get it right. Because what we want is for our children, when
asked where did the movement, the occupation, the resistance, the revolution go, to answer, after looking around them at the world we have so
thoughtfully created, that it is right here, in 'places like this.'"
—Katherine Arnoldi, author of *The Amazing True Story of a Teenage
Single Mom*

"Activist mothers Law and Martens propose that radical movements
interested in winning must welcome parents and their children—the
youngest rabble-rousers. They have created a practical guide for us all
to do just that, but with zero guilt trips and moralizing. *Don't Leave Your
Friends Behind* puts teeth into the slogan 'Another World Is Possible' by
showing us what a healthy left might look like."
—James Tracy coauthor of *Hillbilly Nationalists, Urban Race Rebels,
and Black Power: Community Organizing in Radical Times*

"*Don't Leave Your Friends Behind* is an essential resource for the interdependence revolution in progress. As a queer, chronically ill woman of
color who loves and needs the parents and kids in my communities, I am
hungry for these on-the-ground stories of how parents, allies, comrades,

fam and friends are rewriting the world by refusing to hold mamas, papis, and kids anywhere but at the center of our movements and communities, where we're supposed to be."
—Leah Lakshmi Piepzna-Samarasinha, coeditor of *The Revolution Starts at Home: Confronting Intimate Violence in Activist Communities*

"Finally! *Don't Leave Your Friends Behind* is a resource we have long since needed to make the world we deserve which is full with love, and parents and kids and time and space and intentionally taking care of each other. Get ready for a cooler, more accessible, more possible and purposeful intergenerational movement. Get ready to win!"
—Alexis Pauline Gumbs, Broken Beautiful Press, Eternal Summer of the Black Feminist Mind, and Queer Black Mobile Home Coming Project.

"Activists talk about creating a better world for future generations yet often neglect the needs of children and parents in their midst. *Don't Leave Your Friends Behind* is a poignant, powerful, and much-needed reminder of how movements can raise their own awareness—and that crucial next generation of activists as well."
—Randall Amster, author of *Anarchism Today* and executive director of the Peace and Justice Studies Association

"*Don't Leave Your Friends Behind* is an inspiring call to action for social justice communities globally. It is shows us not only why but how we should not merely 'tolerate' children and parents in our activist communities, it shows, through honest and illuminating stories, that centering them in our communities and movements strengthens our work and our analysis. I cannot wait to be able to hand a copy of this book to many nonparent activist friends and say, 'See, this is a vision of the future that is too beautiful not to struggle for.'"
—Mai'a Williams, editor of *Outlaw Midwives* zine

DON'T LEAVE YOUR FRIENDS BEHIND

DON'T LEAVE YOUR FRIENDS BEHIND

Concrete Ways to Support Families in
Social Justice Movements and Communities

Victoria Law and China Martens

PM Press | 2012

ISBN: 978-1-60486-396-3
Library of Congress Control Number: 2012945336

Interior design by Antumbra Design/Antumbradesign.org
Cover design by Josh MacPhee
Cover illustration by Melanie Cervantes

10 9 8 7 6 5 4 3 2

PM Press
PO Box 23912
Oakland, CA 94623
www.pmpress.org

Printed in the USA.

An earlier version of "Audacious Enough Mama" was originally published on the blog *Fabulosa Mujer*. "Fathering the World" first appeared in *Rad Dad* issue #2. "The Red Crayon" originally appeared in *HipMama* magazine #40. "How to Build Community That Involves Single Parents" was originally published on the blog *Hermana Resist*. "Mami vs. Mommy, Mami'hood vs. Motherhood: What Do Mami Movements Need?" was originally published on the blog *Mamita Mala: One Bad Mami* http://www.lamamitamala.com/blog/?p=401. "A Message from Mamas of Color Rising" originally appeared on the *Mamas of Color Rising* blog: http://mamasofcolorrising.wordpress.com/2010/06/. An earlier version of "Experiencing Critical Resistance 10 (CR10) Through the Children's Program" originally appeared on the SPARK Reproductive Justice NOW website: http://www.sparkrj.org/. "Whose City? KIDZ CITY!" originally appeared in the *Indypendent Reader* #12 (spring/summer 2009). "An Open Letter to Movement Men" was originally published on the website for the Bay Area Childcare collective. "Men Running Childcare" originally appeared on the *London Pro-Feminist Men's Group* blog: http://londonprofeministmensgroup.blogspot.com/2009/04/men-running-child-care.html. "This Poem Is in Honor of Mothers," "Homefulness" and "Un Corazon separado por una frontera" originally appeared in Poor Magazine. "Accessibility" was first published in *Cripchick's Blog* http://blog.cripchick.com/archives/2910.

Contents

Preface   1

Chapter 1: Challenging the Status Quo

Audacious Enough Mama by *Fabiola Sandoval*   9
Fathering the World by *Tomas Moniz*   12
We're Here . . . We're Queer . . . and That's Not All by *Rei*   15
Doing It Together: An Interview with Diana Block on
   Childcare, Movement Support, and Parenting
   Underground by *Victoria Law*   18

Chapter 2: Building Blocks

The Red Crayon by *Jessica Trimbath*   29
La Casita Is Ours! A Conversation with Children in Struggle
   by *Rozalinda Borcilă*   34
New Kids on the Block by *Ramsey Beyer*   45
Lactivists Do It Better: What Radical Parents' Allies Can Learn
   from La Leche League International by *Mariah Boone*   49
The Unfinished Universe by *Darran White Tilghman*   53

Chapter 3: What's Gender, Race, and Class Got to Do with It?

This Poem Is in Honor of Mothers by *Tiny a.k.a. Lisa Gray-Garcia*   61
Is Everyone at the Table? An Interview with Noemi Martinez,
   Fabiola Sandoval, and Maegan "la Mamita Mala" Ortiz—
   Three Single Mother of Color Media Makers by *Victoria Law*
   and China Martens   62
How to Build a Community That Involves Single Parents
   by *Noemi Martinez*   67
Mami vs. Mommy, Mami'hood vs. Motherhood: What Do Mami
   Movements Need? by *Maegan "la Mamita Mala" Ortiz*   69
Support Can Be Conditional When You're Trans or Queer:
   An Interview with Katie Kaput and Jennifer Fichter
   by *Victoria Law*   72

Performing Allyship: Notes from a Queer Migrant Parent by *a de la maza pérez tamayo*   79

On Fear and Commitments by *Mustafa Shukur*   82

Chapter 4: Collective Action

A Message from Mamas of Color Rising and Young Women United: Mother's Day, 2010   91

Reclaim the Commons by *Maxina Ventura*   94

Experiencing Critical Resistance 10 (CR10) Through the Children's Program by *Kate Shapiro*   97

Whose City? KIDZ CITY! by *Sine Hwang Jensen, Harriet Moon Smith, and China Martens*   101

Homefulness by *Tiny, a.k.a. Lisa Gray-Garcia*   105

Mothers Among Us: The Prison Birth Project by *Marianne Bullock*   108

Organizing within an Anarcha-Feminist Childrearing Collective by *CRAP! Collective*   111

An Open Letter to Movement Men by *David Gilbert*   116

Men Running Childcare by *London Pro-Feminist Men's Group*   117

Continuing the Struggle: Lessons Learned from Mothers and Children in Zapatista Communities by *Victoria Law*   119

Chapter 5: Lists, Lessons, and Concrete Tips for Supporting Children and Caregivers

Tips on How to Support Your Friend During Pregnancy by *Jessica Hoffmann*   129

Taking Care of Your Friends Postpartum by *Clayton Dewey*   131

Babyproofing for Punks by *Clayton Dewey*   133

Supporting Your Friend Who Lost Their Newborn Infant by *Mikaela Shafer*   136

Concrete Things You Can Do to Support Parents and Children in Your Scene: Suggestions Brainstormed at La Rivolta!, an Anarcha-Feminist Conference in Boston, 2006   137

Lessons from Planning Radical Childcare by *China Martens*   139

Radical Childcare Collective Start-Up Notes by *Amariah Love*   144

Wizards Around the Rainbow by *Encian Pastel & the Bay Area Childcare Collective*   152

Activities for Children by *Rahula Janowski, China Martens,*
    and Victoria Law   162
Creating Family Space by *Jason Gonzales, Revolutionary*
    Parenting Caucus, and a-parenting listserv   164
Don't Forget Familiez on the Rez! by *Mari Villaluna*   166
Concrete Ways to Support Parents and Children Fighting White
    Supremacy from a Pan-Afrikan Perspective by *Monalisa*
    Lennon Diallo a.k.a. Oluko Lumumba, Agnes Johnson, and
    Mariahadessa Ekere Tallie   167
Holistic First Aid for All Ages by *Traci Picard*   169

Chapter 6: Different Approaches
Taking Community-Building Seriously by *Heather Jackson*   177
Equal Access: Community Childcare for Special Needs
    by *Jennifer Silverman*   180
How Do We Integrate Kids and Adults? What Are Our
    Expectations about Integrating with Each Other as a
    Community? (snippets from a discussion on the a-parenting
    listserv) by *Laura Gyre, Simon Knaphus, and Briana Cavanaugh*   184
Call to Destiny by *A.S. Givens*   187
Supporting Unschooling Families by *Sasha Luci*   193
Ways to Support Single Mothers by *mama raccoon*   196
At My Church, We Call It "Radical Hospitality" by *Coleen Murphy*   198

Chapter 7: Don't Leave Anyone Behind
Accessibility by *Stacey Milbern*   205
Don't Leave Your Mental Health Behind by *Lindsey Campbell*   208
Parental Caregiving and Loss: Ideas for Caregivers and Their
    Allies by *Kathleen McIntyre and Cynthia Ann Schemmer*   211
Un Corazón separado por una frontera/A Heart Separated by a
    Border by *Ingrid DeLeon (*translated by *Carina Lomeli*
    /POOR Magazine)   218
Through All the Transitions: A Duet on Caregiving, Family,
    and Community by *Jessica Mills and Amanda Rich*   221

Contributor Biographies   226
Acknowledgments   234

Preface

Don't Leave Your Friends Behind is a compilation of essays, narratives, and concrete suggestions on ways that social justice communities and movements can support the parents, children, and caregivers in their midst. It is a book for everyone, particularly activists and organizers without children of their own, who would like to become better allies to the parents and children in their communities.

This book is the culmination of a seven-year collaboration between two radical mothers, Vikki Law and China Martens. The origins of *Don't Leave Your Friends Behind* go back to 2003 when we first met and co-facilitated a workshop (for parents) on creating a radical parents' support network at Baltimore's Anarchist Bookfair. At first, we attempted to hold our workshop inside the building where the bookfair took place. When we realized that parents were having problems keeping their small children occupied, we moved the workshop onto the grass outside so that the children could play. One mother volunteered to do childcare, so that the other parents could talk and listen without missing the discussion to chase their children. However, this meant she missed the workshop entirely. The parents who attended all stated that they had very little support from their radical communities; they often felt forced to rely on mainstream resources that were neither meeting all of their needs nor reflecting their values. Our conversation with disheartened, burnt-out, and tired parents was a stark contrast with the carefree-looking faces of attendees without children who were joyfully walking by, sometimes smiling at the children as they passed. They had the energy we needed! The radical parents needed the support of the predominantly childless crowd who were coming and going all around us.

After that event, we realized the need to give workshops for the whole community, especially those without children of their own. *Don't Leave Your Friends Behind* evolved from this experience.

In 2006, the anarcha-feminist conference *La Rivolta!* invited us to facilitate a workshop on why those interested in anarchism and/or feminism should be concerned about mothers' and children's issues and how they can support the families in—or slowly being pushed out of—their movements. That one workshop led to several others—in Montreal, Baltimore, and Providence—that same year. Since then, we have presented or participated in more than a dozen workshops and discussions at various conferences, bookfairs, and gatherings. The continued interest in our talks illustrates the growing awareness among social justice organizers of the need to support families as well as the growing realization that they may not necessarily know how to do so.

Over the years, we have engaged in many conversations on how to increase community support with different people and in different locations. We have heard from single moms struggling to balance childrearing and political involvement with little to no recognition or support from their childless peers. We have heard from mothers who take action to save their children's futures and are then criticized by both spouses and community for neglecting "family duties." We have heard from fathers who do not leave their children behind to save the world, despite peer pressure to do so, but instead extend their fathering to others in the world. We have heard from parents of children with developmental disabilities and (adult) disability justice activists; from trans parents and doulas supporting incarcerated mothers. We also heard from teachers and childcare workers. We have heard, time and again, about the many ways that race, gender, class, geography, custody agreements, and health, among other factors, impact families and children. Not all groups of parents struggle equally.

Nor do all groups of parents and caregivers speak or write in the same way. As editors, we have done our best to keep the writers' original voices intact. As you leaf through the pages, you'll notice British spellings from contributors in the UK and Australia, the intermingling of Spanish mixed with English words and word choices and spellings that may seem unconventional. In all cases, there are intentions behind the words, from Maegan Ortiz's use of Spanish peppered into her essay to Tiny's poetic license in splicing the words "messed" and "with" into a new word: "withed."

We also had conversations with each other as radical mothers of two different generations. Vikki's daughter was two and China's was fifteen when we first met. We have different life experiences: Vikki is a mother of color raising her child in predominantly white anarchist circles in NYC. She recognized that the support she received from her community enabled her to stay involved in political work. China is a single mother who has moved often, always looking for better environments in which to raise her child. She returned to Baltimore, where she and her daughter have lived since 2001. While she feels blessed for the support of family, friends, and community, she has still experienced the poverty resulting from insufficient support.

Regardless of the differences in our lives and experiences, we recognize that, despite its rhetoric of creating works based on solidarity and mutual aid, anarchist and radical movements mimic, to a degree, the greater society's unreasonable expectations of parents, especially mothers, and children. When a radical woman becomes a mother, she often finds herself left behind by her mostly childless peer group. Various social justice movements and radical left philosophies challenge us to create personal and social change but often provide no support for mothers who try to do so.

Readers may also notice that the stories in this anthology reflect the racial divide that often occurs in social justice organizing. This reflects the world that we live in despite rhetoric that we live in a "post-racial" era. We recognize these divides and have striven to include the diversity of voices across these divides without creating a laundry list of identities that tokenizes more than recognizes. No one book can cover everyone and everything. Similarly, readers should not assume that any one person or group's experience is universally shared. *Don't Leave Your Friends Behind* should not be seen as the all-encompassing book. It is an opening to a conversation and a reminder to stay open and mindful to others' stories, needs, and experiences.

How do we support the different needs of our children, their caretakers, and our communities in an environment where access to resources is so unequal?

We need to refocus on community support. Nuclear families are a recent invention and have not historically been the way children have been raised. We recognize that even two-parent families, as well as all those who do caretaking work, also need support. Respecting, valuing, and sharing caregiving work helps diffuse the stress and builds a healthier community for all. We all need to learn how to take care of others as well as ourselves, how to nurture and how to share physical and emotional responsibilities.

How do we create new, non-hierarchical structures of support and mutual aid, and include all ages in the struggle for social justice? There are many books on parenting, but few on being a good community member and a good ally to parents, caregivers, and children as we collectively build a strong all-ages culture of resistance. Any group of parents will tell you how hard their struggles are and how they are left out, but no book focuses on how allies can address issues of caretakers' and children's oppression. Isolated by age within an individualistic, capitalist culture, many well-intentioned childless activists don't interact with young people on a regular basis and don't know how. *Don't Leave Your Friends Behind* provides them with the resources and support to get started. Together we can build a better world without leaving anyone behind.

One
CHALLENGING THE STATUS QUO

We're tired of activists wondering where all the parents are when we're sitting at home with no money, no transportation, and no childcare. . . We expect to struggle against the world; we don't expect to struggle in our own community. —Revolutionary Anarchist Mom and Baby League, "Allies, Who Aren't," *Earth First! Journal* (2003)

"Why should I care? I didn't choose to have children" is a common refrain among many individuals without children in social justice movements. This question ignores the connections linking all systems of oppression. When any one group disregards the needs of any other group, it perpetuates the inequities of the larger society. The myth of independence over interdependence is a capitalism-induced illusion. We all rely on each other and we all have different needs (which also change across our lifespan). How do we build the world we want to see if we refuse to recognize and support each other's access to meet basic needs?

When movements and communities fail to collectively support having children in their spaces and events, they perpetuate and reinforce the belief that families need to turn back to the dominant system—with all its privilege, lack of privilege, patriarchy, exploitation, inequality, and injustice—to take care of their needs. Many families struggle to build communities of resistance and to fight injustice while, at the same time, feeling that these same "communities" dismiss, devalue, or don't even consider their needs and the needs of their children.

How do we create new, non-hierarchical systems of support and mutual aid? How can we include people of all ages in our struggles for social justice? We can begin by listening to the stories and experiences of those on the front lines.

Audacious Enough Mama
Fabiola Sandoval

Yesterday, I took my baby to a meeting with staff members from the County to discuss the creation of an emergency housing access center for the growing number of families in downtown LA. With baby in my lap, I silently disagreed while feeling audacious and political just by taking my child into this "setting."

The space alone had me quiet. Everyone talked over each other during the heated fundamental "bigger picture" moments. Upper management titles were propped up around the fancy wooden table, an intimidating sight. In a conference room of professionals without children present, I remained silent.

My silence seeped in the fear of getting kicked out, or thrown an uncomfortable dirty look or a whisper, due to a small child on my lap. (For the record, if she screams for more than a few seconds, I leave any room.)

Being a mom in public with a toddler is trying, especially in places like meetings, trainings, conferences, and events. I am always worried about getting in the way of an anti-child person, getting a disgusted look, hearing a remark that will bother the hell out of me and have me thinking it through the next time. Making a trip to an un–family friendly setting is an act that requires a certain "I don't give a ****" personality that, on occasion, I might have. Usually, though, leaving the house is an act reserved for child-friendly places.

I've been told that I'm too worried that my child will disrupt something and that I've allowed this to affect my presence, voice, and input. My five senses are always divided in staying attentive as a mother and as a productive member of a meeting/training/event. Staying on top of both is exhausting and keeps me nervous despite the fact that I've been taking my daughter into those strictly adult places for a year now. This level of caretaker worried-the-hell-out-of-inconveniencing-other-folks has largely preoccupied me to the point of constantly leaving a room. Even when I'm on the agenda in a meeting, I give priority to not inconveniencing childfree people. I've been called out for not taking risks by disagreeing, for not contributing, for not resisting to leave a room while *fabniña* relaxes a bit. I will often say something after a training: write my thoughts down to then share after a committee meeting, only to then be asked why I didn't share with the rest from the start.

My experiences have given me awareness of the very real power dynamics between individuals with and without children: awareness of the stigma associated with mothering, and the risks of oppression for caretakers with small children in public spaces.

In the meeting with the County professionals, folks talked about getting families (meaning mothers of color who have one to three children) out of homelessness, but not once broached the idea of creating affordable long-term housing; no one even mentioned the possibility that "the need-to-be-fixed-and-helped crowd" can and should remain in an invested community instead of being pushed out. Why do Work, Live and Play revitalization plans mean high-end lofts for young urban professionals without children who are able to pay $2,500 in rent while single women, men, and families that have been on "skid row" must resort to transitional shelters and emergency beds for months and years? Not once were these radical ideas considered by those who want to alleviate homelessness and affordable housing dilemmas. In that moment, I hated reform to the bone. I walked out of the room and dared someone to question children in public spaces, my "just let someone mess with me" attitude in development.

I have also attended other, more grassroots community housing rights events. These groups are mostly Salvadorian, Mexican, Guatemalan, Honduran, and include one or two families from South America. There are children at these meetings, yes, and quite a number of them. Both of these groups are working towards housing equity and tenant rights. Most of the folks that come out to the events, *convivios* (get-togethers), and leadership development meetings are women, specifically women of color, who are mothers. They take their children everywhere.

There are also the older folk and the non-parents who dislike having the children around. At the first meeting I attended, there was a critique about the children being noisy, annoying, rambunctious, wild, making it hard to concentrate; one or two folks were pissed. Now, part of the problem was that they didn't want children around at all. The other problem was that women who were active weren't paying attention to their children. Not once was someone willing to sit with the children with colors, paints, paper, etc., in another room because of the gendered and low value of that work.

Even more women and children were present at the second event I attended. The children were in a room with a woman who was playing, coloring, painting, drawing, and reading with them. The "women's work" that appeared to have low value in the last group was valued in this situation. Since the childcare responsibilities of the group were recognized and rotated, these women are able to be the fiercest active leaders in a community fighting gentrification. They have not dropped off the radar because they are mothers. They organize themselves to adapt to the phases of mothering young children.

The victories that I have seen at a grassroots, working class level, from the bus riders' union and garment workers to major land and job agreements, have been from mothers and folks who aren't against mothers or children. Mothers are a proven force in grassroots victory in our communities at home and abroad. They are essential to any movement that is trying to create change in the name of justice.

I feel that it is time I begin advocating my own work-in-progress, publicly confident, mama-with-child-on-her-hip presence in my "activism" work—work that I do with very "progressive" feminist women who have the means to leave their children at home or women who are not mothers at all. I need to start calling out the societal age-ism towards children when I see it and when it is directed home. It is time for the unapologetic "I don't need your permission to have my child present on my lap or hip, or crawling/running around" thought to gain strength. It is time for me to proudly parent in public as I facilitate, disagree, and give input in heated discussions, even while fabniña arches her back, pushes her legs in the air, and screeches in protest to be released and run out of the room from the eyes and ears of the children-less crowd.

Fathering the World
Tomas Moniz

Of all the pictures of the devastation wrought by Hurricane Katrina, one mesmerized and overwhelmed me, seeming to contain all that I wanted to believe about fathers—no, not just fathers, but men in our lives. The picture transcended the racist media spin; it eased the pain of the decimated street scenes and moments of panic. One man. One child, a child not his. The man was wading through water, holding the child as if this was the most important thing he could do, as though not just the child's life but his own life depended on their safe arrival. He asked no questions about whose child it was; there was no need to ascertain ownership or ask permission. There were no pathetic excuses about needing to wait and see, to assess things, like we kept hearing from "men in charge." He knew: I help this child and I help myself. I help all of us get by. There was such humanity in his arms, in the determination in his eyes. It spoke to me as the epitome of "fathering," of caring for not just about our immediate family but about all our relations. I stared, reminded of how much of an impact we can have on the children in our lives, how easy it is to overlook, to forget, to deprioritize others as we take care of our own.

A few weeks ago, I heard a story about a young boy who has been in my life for years now, a boy whose own father has not been around, a father whom I cannot find a way to forgive nor understand his willingness to abandon, like something disposable, his offspring. Well, this boy was with his mother, and was looking into one of those mirrors that elongates and distorts its reflection. He stared at himself, made a muscle, and said, "Look, it's almost as big as Tom's." When I heard how he compared his reflection to me, I again realized, as with the picture, how fathering is something all men do, whether we want to or not, whether we are prepared for it or not. So it is incumbent upon us to think through who we are and how we affect others, especially the children in our lives. And this is true, whether we are parents or not. Around the same time, I had an argument about this with a male non-parent who said it's not his responsibility to know how to be around kids. He believes this because of the silence around parenting, around the public's perceptions of children being seen not heard, of good behavior equaling good kids, of ownership ("If it ain't my kid, why should I care?"). I have friends who take diversity training courses to be prepared to work with people of color, enroll in permaculture classes for the coming demise of civilization, but seem unconcerned about working with parents or kids, outreaching to parents or kids, or creating ways to make actions, spaces, conferences parent- and child-friendly. This silence and inaction is a failure. It's unforgivable.

I feel that we men are particularly at fault. There is a silence among men about fathering. I experience this as I talk with men about fathering; they are excited yet scared, nervous about making mistakes. Most are dying to parent in ways that many of us weren't fathered. But there are very few role models, and the society we live in disempowers men to break from the prescribed role of the male parent, the role that supports patriarchy, capitalism, hierarchy, and authoritarianism. Unfortunately, many women collude in this process of disempowering male experiences of parenting. Women, it seems, are often cast in roles to speak about parenting because somehow they are better with kids, more sensitive, more nurturing, because they are women while men can only speak about being proud, being happy and supportive. Or, even worse, they can address only issues of discipline. It has been very difficult to get men to commit to writing something about their ideas, their approach, their fears or experiences of parenting. They feel shamed, silenced, or not knowledgeable enough.

This must end. The diversity of fathering is multitude, while the prescribed role remains largely singular.

What can we learn from a gay father about discussing sexuality with our daughters? I want to hear it. What can a working class father share with us about fighting patriarchy in the household while still having to struggle with a nine-to-five job? We need to hear it. How does a white father discuss race with his white son or his biracial daughter? Every single one of us can benefit from hearing that story.

For the last few months, I have been going to zine fairs and trying to get the word out about *Rad Dad*.[1] I am puzzled by the responses when

---

1. This was written during the zine's early days. *Rad Dad* is now a book (PM Press, 2011) as well as a zine.

I say it's a zine on fathering, on how men impact the world and the children around them. Most people smile and say, "I ain't a dad" or "I don't know anyone who is." When I ask if there are children in their lives or if they are uncles or if they are thinking about being a parent, most just smile and say something like, "Well, I'll deal with that later. Those things don't relate to me now."

Tell that to the man who picked up the child, held her close to his chest and waded out in the waters that were destroying the very place he lived. How we relate to our own children, how we connect with the kids and teenagers on our blocks and in our communities is analogous to how we envision a better world, a more compassionate, loving, creative world. If we curtail that relationship, as we are doing, we will continue to live our lives surrounded by levees that cannot hold.

We're Here. . . We're Queer. . . and That's Not All

Rei

My name is Rei. I live in Australia with my little queer poly tribe, and we do our best to provide radical parenting and education for our kids Medea (7) and Theo (8). The condensed version of our story is that we try to parent and educate them in a way that is sex- and body-positive and allows them as much supported autonomy as possible while encouraging them to challenge hetero/gender normativity and giving them the tools to critically evaluate all the -isms and norms and rules they encounter. We are making it up as we go along and there has been, and will be, much trial and error. But that is ultimately what we aim for.

There are many intersections within my tribe . . . I'm a biracial genderqueer sex worker and student. One of my partners is a high femme *pâtissière* and the other is a beautiful butch painter and musician. One of the kids' dads is a bisexual circus teacher, and his boyfriend is a queer social worker and performer. Our extended network of chosen kin is just as multifaceted. I tell you all this not because we are poster children for diversity, but because we *aren't*. Families that transgress what is commonly accepted as normativity are everywhere. But they are just out of sight, marginalized, ignored. Neo-liberal, supposedly non-homophobic, attempts at acceptance do occasionally surface. I read in the paper yesterday that "evidence is mounting (that) children from same-sex parents are academically as capable as children of heterosexual couples." There is not enough room in this essay to fully explore everything that is wrong with this headline; suffice to say that it illustrates how far we have to go. That article is as close as my family comes to being acknowledged in mainstream media and, still, they aren't even talking about us. Maybe in the future when the term "Gender Diverse Co-Parents" comes into vogue, we will have the absurd right to be judged based on our children's grades along with gay and lesbian parents.

I cite the above example because it highlights the pressure on queer parents to provide evidence that their lives and choices are valid and not damaging. Not only our children's grades, but their identities, physical appearance, demeanour, knowledge-base, and life experiences would be evaluated harshly by the majority were the spotlight turned on us. No matter that they are healthy, happy, and remarkably self-aware; no matter that they reap huge rewards from being a part of an extended network of adults who love and support them. Many people still believe gay and lesbian parenting to be inherently harmful and deviant. What then of the family and system of parental ethics I have described? Can't you just hear the cry *Children at Risk!* In deference to this constant discourse of "risk" and children, we use slogans of the "Same but Different" ilk. *We're Just Like You!* the same sex marriage campaigners insist, as though queer relationships are acceptable only as long as they are homogenised versions of the straight social paradigm. Oh, and the kid's grades stay up. Where does that leave us and the many others like us?

Where does it leave our kids? Our seven-year-old identifies as an "it" and our eight-year-old is a pink-mohawked, campiest creature on two legs. One of our kids currently has a boyfriend *and* a girlfriend. When the national anthem is sung at school functions, one of them sits down as a conscientious objector; the other one loves to sing anything, anywhere. On holidays, they go to Mardi Gras and Pride March. We all still bathe together; in summer we sleep naked. When either of them asks questions about sex, sexuality, bodies, relationships (and anything else), we answer them. Honestly. Even when that takes time and is confronting or difficult to break down so that they can understand. We don't have TV but they are allowed to read anything in the house. If they want to read something with content that might be new or potentially problematic they have to have an adult on hand to answer questions but other than that, we're anti-censorship. These are some of the practical results of our parental ethics and engagement with the kids. They are random examples meant to illustrate some of the ways we choose to do things differently. That these choices should be assessed as problematic, as putting our kids at risk, is indicative of current dominant politics of sexual fear, hysteria, and censorship. In such a climate, the way we live and parent is radical. But it doesn't feel like that to us. Not to our kids either—not yet anyway. It's just normal. But it is abnormal according to the status quo and, in light of our queerness, even more unacceptable. We *do* do things differently and our happy, healthy kids are fluent and comfortable with ideas and behaviours that many other children their age only experience in the context of shame, ambiguity, and prejudice.

If we were a mum/dad/kids unit, we would be trusted with far more autonomy in the raising of our children and if we transgressed, no one would suggest that it was because we were heterosexual or use our unconventionality as evidence that straight people shouldn't have children. But we aren't, and we don't, and the wonderful queerness of our tribe is evidence against its own validity in the eyes of many.

To other families in the margins—respect and solidarity.

To allies and friends—speaking for myself, one thing I need from you is validation. The world at large does not tell me I am a great parent, does not tell me that it knows I try my best. It does not encourage me to continue to try and challenge gender/hetero normative discourses in the way that I parent. It does not support me in giving my kids information and autonomy. It does not tell me that I can be all the things that I am and be a parent, too. I'm sure all parents doubt and worry, but not all parents have their fundamental right to *be* parents challenged and questioned and examined and afforded criteria. This lack of validation erodes confidence and breeds isolation. When you encounter parents and kids in your communities, take whatever time you have to listen and give positive feedback. Thank them for doing what they do. If we don't parent and educate in a radical way, then long-term change is virtually impossible. Recognising this and according respect and support to the families who are making change happen, could have a huge impact on the radical community's ability to regenerate and sustain itself. And you might just make someone's day.

Doing It Together: An Interview with Diana Block on Childcare, Movement Support, and Parenting Underground

Victoria Law

In 1985, Diana Block became a mother. Two weeks later, her partner found a surveillance device in their car. Block, her two-week-old son, and her five companions—all of whom were active in the struggle for Puerto Rican independence—fled their lives in Los Angeles and spent the next decade living underground. In her memoir *Arm the Spirit*, Diana Block chronicles thirteen years of parenting her two children while keeping their real identities and lives secret, trying to stay true to their political beliefs, and watching for the FBI.

In April of 2009, I interviewed Diana Block after a panel we were on together at Left Forum (an academic-activist conference that did not provide childcare).

What were your pre-escape visions of motherhood? How did you envision balancing motherhood and clandestinity?

I think a lot of times no one can really anticipate what being a mother is. I just saw it as we would be; Tony would just be part of our group. We would try to be parents to the best of our ability even though we were doing clandestine work and that, like everything else in our lives, we'd have to figure it out as it came up because there was no formula that we could really study. For years, I'd been part of childcare teams as part of Prairie Fire organizing committee. Our childcare teams really were seen as part of our political work and the structure of our organization. I knew that in our smaller group everyone was going to help take care of Tony and that wasn't an individual parenting thing. I had also been around kids all my life and helped care for them. It wasn't like I felt I was well prepared to be a mother, but it wasn't like children were a mystery to me. So I think that at a certain point we just jumped in and said, this is what we want to do and we'll figure it out as it comes along.

So you're saying that children were more present and more welcome in the '70s than they are today, say at Left Forum?

[Laughs] Well, yes and no. It was a big struggle, like many things were. I think the women's movement and women's groups did place a demand on the Left to actually take the issue of childcare up and in some pockets of different groups that happened, but it definitely was a struggle. One of the instances in the book that I talk about is when I went to the first West Coast Lesbian Conference and there wasn't childcare. These were lesbians and yet their awareness or consciousness of the issue of childcare was not very progressive, in my opinion. That was the way I first met Karen, my future companion in clandestine organizing. She was standing up and berating the organizers of the lesbian conference for not having set up childcare at the conference. So within Prairie Fire, which was the group that I later became part of, as did Karen, many of us made a big struggle that we had to incorporate childcare. And I think that is different from many groups today; it's very unfortunate that in some ways it's gone backward. I don't know what to say about that except that, like many other things, there was a backlash. Maybe not a conscious backlash, but a reversion, and I think that nowadays more fathers do childcare, but what's different is that there aren't the same group collectives that are responsible for the childcare. And that is one of the most positive aspects, in terms of parenting, that that organization and that period offered. It wasn't without problems; there's never any social innovation that can be smooth. There's always some issue and maybe that's why some people went back to being in a more nuclear arrangements, but from my point of view, it was really a progressive experiment and it worked in many ways, especially for mothers who were single parents and wanted to do political work. It was a resource and structure that allowed them to do that work. There was childcare available five nights a week in general and people could make their schedules based on when there would be childcare. And it was not only care, per se, but also input and discussion and help figuring things out about the kids. That's where it was more contradictory because, like many things on the Left, people could become arrogant and opinionated. And I feel that the mother, the parent, has to have the final say and not be intimidated by everyone else's great ideas. Because every parent is going to do it differently. So that was the downside. But, having said that, we also recognized at some point that it was a downside and tried to correct that. But, overall, I think it was a wonderful structure in terms of having people committed to helping to take care of children.

This is what you said about the June 1973 First West Coast Lesbian Conference at UCLA (with 2,000 attendees and no childcare): "My very first memory of Karen (who later was part of our underground collective) was when she took the mic at the conference and berated the organizers for not providing childcare and implicitly equating motherhood with patriarchal cooptation" What was the response of the conference organizers?

I don't think it was very positive. That's not to indict that particular conference; it's certainly not to indict lesbian organizing in that period, because if anything, it was only because there was some openness that there was the ability to make that criticism. At that point, one of the early struggles in the lesbian movement was whether motherhood was in some way patriarchally defined. Looking back, it seems impossible that people really could have thought that, but here, too, with hindsight, you could say, "okay, but women were trying to break out of certain molds and explore what was totally 'natural' and what the options were." To be a person who didn't have children as a woman was extremely negative in the society as a whole. So people were trying to break with the notion that people had to have children to be genuinely women, and that was part of the Second Wave feminism, including lesbian women who felt that they wanted to make the choice not to be mothers. So, in pushing to make that a reality, I think that people went overboard for a period, but obviously that has been corrected and has changed over time. But there were edges of people who said, "We don't want to be responsible for the children." Women could make that choice [to have children], but they did not want to be responsible as a conference if women made that choice. So, I don't think that there were extremely good responses at that particular conference. But in general, I think that the lesbian and gay movement, over time, changed and became very in the forefront of figuring out how to care for children in different ways. And many of the people in Prairie Fire were lesbians and gay men, so it was definitely something that, in our organization, we tried to take on in the framework of lesbian and gay movement.

How, if at all, did this influence your vision of motherhood?

At the time, I was glad that she [Karen] did it. I was very glad because I didn't feel in the position to do it [make that critique of the conference]. I didn't have a child, she had a child, and that was also something that wasn't conventional at the time. Looking back at it, this was the first arrangement of that kind that I knew of at the time, that many people probably knew of at the time: she and her partner Jody and another woman, it was like three parents for a girl. It wasn't a formal adoption, but it was a consensual arrangement with that child's parents. It worked for everyone: it worked for the parents, it worked for them, it worked for the daughter for the time being. It was the first time I had seen such a non-traditional parenting arrangement and I thought it was great; I was very impressed that they were able to do that. It was a number of years before we in Prairie Fire adopted the childcare collectives, but it was certainly one piece of influencing, of thinking about different kinds of childcare arrangements.

Was childcare the norm or usually expected at conferences back then?

It varied. As there were more and more struggles and issues made of it, it became more commonplace. Even at events, and I remember that there were more events than conferences (thank god), there was always childcare at events. This was something that people signed up for—we had to do security, we had to do tabling, we had to have people at the door, and we had to have childcare. One of the components when we planned an event is that we had to have childcare in it.

Today, well, I know that Critical Resistance had it at their conference and there are certain, I would say, more radical sectors of the movement where that is an expectation. There was a certain period where it was normalized to have childcare at various movement activities and that is not the case anymore.

I remember when Siu Loong was little. I felt very isolated from the movement because there wasn't that same amount of support and I would read about some injustice and think, "I really wanna do something! Oh no, I can't because I have a small child and no support system." So I was wondering if you had encountered that frustration, too, especially since you were parenting small children while living underground and cut off from a larger political community.

There was that frustration, too, but I did have a group of other adults who took care of my child a lot. In addition to the daycare, Tony had six adults who loved him and took care of him. I didn't ever feel, in that sense, that I was just the person who he had to depend on. I had an immediate framework and I couldn't have asked for more support in the day-to-day. It would have been very different if I had been by myself and having to figure out everything around him or if I had been undergoing a very difficult separation from the other parent or there were fights over how much other people were going to care for the child. That gave me an amazing foundation. I think that's true for our entire history—we were able to survive politically and remain committed activists after many years because we all were doing it together. We didn't have a big split or a horrible fight—we had fights, I don't want to romanticize it, but nothing led to divisions where we couldn't remain working together.

After [your partner] Claude went to prison, you wrote: "How could I reconcile being forty-six years old and a single parent with my desire to recreate the time when politics had shaped my daily existence? How could I find political work that made sense to me, while accepting the fact that I was not available for meetings every night of the week and acknowledging that I craved some space for writing and reflection?" This seems to be the dilemma facing most, if not all, mothers who wish to remain politically active. What recommendations and words of advice would you have for them?

I feel like one thing is that this society likes formulas and how-to books and things like that. There is no formula. For any politically active, thoughtful mother, they have to figure it out for themselves. There are no easy solutions. If you're trying to change things, you have to come up with complicated solutions. And that goes on the personal level as well as on the political level. You can't just figure out an arena where you don't have contradictions. That's not what the world is.

Having said that . . . I tried to do things. I was probably too driven. I tried to do too much in that early period, but it was very important for me. I really wanted to be part of that political activity. So I probably went to more meetings than maybe was the best for my children, but I found ways of getting support. That's the other thing. People, mothers, need support and I don't know how people can find it, but I think that making . . . not demands in the negative way . . . but trying to find people who are in one's circle who are open to the idea of being supportive is important. I still had the framework that Prairie Fire had set up years before, so there were people who became part of my childcare support network and took care of Leila and Tony when I came back, so that was definitely an incredible help for me. Not every mother has that, but I think that finding other people who are politically conscious and who will find the need for that is really important. And just figuring out your own balance. People who have careers figure it out. Of course, those people are usually more privileged, have many resources, but I think women, often mothers, have more capacity to do various things if they push themselves and others around them.

Two
BUILDING BLOCKS

I wonder what it must have been like, what dignity it must have conferred on children of the Iroquois confederacy that any child over three was welcome to speak about matters of group importance in the tribal council. —Aurora Levins Morales, *Medicine Stories* (Cambridge, MA: South End Press, 1998)

What if our movements understood that families fighting the status quo need support from their peers and communities? What would our events and spaces look like if organizers reached out to include and engage children in their projects and programs? What does support for a truly multigenerational world look like?

Resistance can take many forms and sizes: In some instances, people have made seemingly small gestures that have helped save a caregiver's immediate patience and sanity. Others build on years' worth of community organizing and plan activities with children as part of their social justice work while still others support and learn from activism led by youth. Each step, small or large, is a victory; each movement is made up of many such building blocks. We all need to start somewhere.

The Red Crayon
Jessica Trimbath

Today at the Novum Pharmaceutical Research Center, everything went as well as expected. Poor women, mostly of color, sat in the waiting room sipping at free water bottles, waiting for the piss test while they argued with their boyfriends over their cell phones. *I can't pick him up. I won't be done until five. I ask you to watch the kids this one time and . . .*

We stared hungry-eyed at the big zeros on the consent form under the section title: *How much will I receive upon completion of this study?* We watched each other walk in with suspicious looks as white, rich women caught their husbands cheating on the Lifetime movie of the week playing on the TV above the clock. *What a dog*, someone commented as the shameless man kissed his young lover on the porch of his summer house. *I'd cut his dick off*, somebody agreed and we chuckled, probably subconsciously thinking of the invasive procedures that awaited us.

Test Drug: Levonorgestrel/Ethinyl Estradiol

It's hard to know what you are worth. A veteran guinea pig explains to a new girl that here, they pay for your blood. The more blood withdrawals they take, the higher the check. They pay for your blood and a clean pussy because those are hard to come by. *But no*, she reassures her kindly, *the pap-smears don't hurt.*

Like hell they don't, I think and I know.

Possible Side Effects: Breast Tenderness, Vomiting, Vaginal Discharge, Blood Clots in Legs or Lungs, Anxiety.

We are all here for the same reason: we are poor. There is no way around it. Her knock-off bag isn't fooling anybody. My wisdom teeth are raging in my gums, trying to break free from under my molars. Impacted.

That means surgery and that's my soul without insurance. I just have to suffer the chronic headaches and nausea until I can't stand on my own and a good friend carries me against my will to the emergency room where they will tell me coldly that I have to go see a dentist. I plan on putting half of this study check away for my teeth. I plan to but I know I won't and I know the other girls have heavier worries than me. We are not doing this for science. Science isn't doing this for any of us. We are being bought and sold like laboratory rats, just as helpless, except we get to eat take-out Boston Market on the first night of confinement and we get to rent horror films to watch on the big leather couches in the middle of the night while they call us in single-file to take our blood for the tenth time that day.

It is very dangerous *to withhold information concerning your medical condition.*

Last time I didn't weigh enough to get accepted. Today my blood pressure is too low. They take me down a long hallway to a tiny room with bad paintings of oceans and docks on the wall. The examiner asks me a hundred questions about my medical history. Have I ever broken a bone? I laugh and say yes, when I was six, thinking she wouldn't care because it was so long ago. She smiles and then the humanity vanishes and she begins typing in the details: how long ago was that? Was I casted?

She continues and I keep lying.

Any history of psychiatric illness?

No.

Any depression, anxiety, or mood swings?

No.

Do you use drugs or alcohol?

No.

She eyes me suspiciously.

Please Note: Whichever method of birth control you choose, remember that, aside from abstinence, all birth control methods sometimes fail.

Most of the women here are mothers. Their children writhe and wriggle impatiently in the hard chairs. The mothers are stressed and the nurses stare at them like they have committed some grave *faux pas* in bringing their children to a medical facility. The mothers look ashamed and angry. They get annoyed with every question their kids ask. They grab whatever the kids touch and snatch it from their hands. The children are gorgeous, so many shades of beautiful baby skin and the sound of their diapers squishing in their jumpers makes me smile as they make their way around the room, searching for anything to satisfy their brilliant curiosity.

I get nervous. I can't imagine how boring this place must be for children, how unbearable it must be for poor mothers. Why do people react to other people's children as if they are diseases? Why doesn't this place have a kid section or room with toys and crayons? Our society is at once anti-choice and anti-mother. We shame women for needing abortions, saying life is precious and babies are valuable, yet we offer no relief to mothers in shopping areas, in doctors' offices, in welfare lines. Where are a mother's accessibility rights? A mother carrying and managing three little ones while trying to buy groceries should be considered disabled insomuch as she should be given the option of using a fun cart designed to carry groceries and entertain kids at once. She should be able to leave her kids in a safe and clean room full of toys and other children where kind, specially trained caregivers will be at all times ensuring their well-being. She should, at the very least, not be stared at and silently shamed as if her having babies was a crude, irresponsible act of bad moral judgment.

The tension in the waiting room rises as the kids get more bored and the mothers get angrier. Last time I was here, a mother hit her son in the face and I stood up and started yelling, telling her I was going to call the police. I threw down the words *child abuse* as easily as she threw down *white bitch* and we stood there screaming at each other, both of us tired and triggered, two adult children, survivors of abuse and addiction, trying so hard to prove to the other one that we weren't the ones, that we were hard, that we weren't really this way. In the meantime, the smacked child's wails grew to a deafening pierce while his siblings hated me with their whole bodies, standing beside their mother's strong legs, staring up at me with accusatory eyes.

You don't know how it is! she said sharply and she was right.

You're right. I don't, I admitted, *but I got hit when I was little and I can't stand to see that shit.*

She looked at me and we didn't say anything. The nurses came out and told us to knock it off or we were leaving and we wouldn't be allowed back. The last part shut us up right quick. We needed Novum. Novum didn't need us.

Later on, I saw her in the study and, as happens with girls who throw down spit and blood and curses together, we had a strange lingering respect for one another and we eventually got to talking. She was ashamed of what she did. I was ashamed of the way I acted. We both laughed and apologized and became good friends for the weekend. We exchanged numbers, but neither of us ever called the other.

To be eligible for this study, you must NOT be pregnant, trying to get pregnant, or lactating and/or breastfeeding.

Today I came prepared. I have crayons and paper in my bag and as soon as the kids start crying, I bring them out slowly, sitting down cross-legged on the floor while the kids suck up their sobs and start staring at me. I smile at them. Their mothers look at me like I'm crazy, but as soon as they see their kids smiling, they smile too. I look at them and ask if it's all right. They say yes. The kids run off the chairs and join me on the floor, grabbing crayons with fat little fists, announcing proudly what they are going to draw.

We sit like this for a while. I am premenstrual, which means I am in contact with the core of crying at the center of every cell in my body and I have to hold back tears every time a child draws a fat smiling sun above a beautiful house with a yard because I know it's something they can't have and they are so innocent and loving and hopeful. I fall in love with each one and when I leave, I wave and they wave and I want to grab the nurses and demand to know why some people are so fucking poor while others have everything they could never need. Why will these children lose so much and learn to be so bitter and live as if they aren't worth anything? Who's to blame? Why is everyone on the TV white when most of the world isn't? Why do I have to whore myself out like this to pay for my teeth?

Why aren't there any crayons or toys for the children that come here with their mothers? I ask the director of the study who's sitting behind the glass in the lobby.

She stutters a little and flips her pages and says she doesn't know. I explain very smilingly and kindly that I think it would be a great way to make the place more comfortable for everyone. She agrees. She says she will look into it.

I walk away carrying my crayon. It's not sharp like a labrys or strong like a fist. It's subtle. It's blood red. Today, it's my little symbol of victory.

La Casita Is Ours! A Conversation with Children in Struggle

Rozalinda Borcilă

On September 13, 2010, a group of mothers and their school children occupied the field house of Whittier Elementary School in Chicago. This is a small building on school grounds, known as La Casita, or the little house, which has long been used by parents and children as a community center, ad-hoc childcare co-op, base for ESL classes and safe space for children to gather and do homework while waiting for parents. It belongs to the school, but it is also a kind of community home.

Academically, the Whittier school is unique: it is a dual-language English-Spanish program developed by dedicated and progressive teachers, many of whom come from bilingual programs that have been dismantled in other schools. In terms of facilities, however, it suffers the same organized abandonment as most public schools in Chicago's poor communities of color. It is badly in need of repair, basic upgrades, and supplies. It is also one of the 150 public schools in the city with no library. Parents had been organizing for years, and as a result of their efforts they received written assurances from city officials that $1.4 million in Tax Increment Financing (TIF) funds would be used for the renovation of the Whittier school, with community and parent input into the renovation process. Cynically, Chicago Public Schools (CPS) initiated a plan to use $354,000 of the allocated funds for the demolition of La Casita, the field house that had been the home base of parent organizing efforts.[1] The official narrative was that the field house was in poor

---

1. Reportedly this plan was in conjunction with a backdoor deal that would sell the lot to a local private high school in need of a new soccer field. When this plan was exposed, CPS and city officials cited the need for more "green space" in Pilsen, the predominately Mexican neighborhood where La Casita is located. Mainstream media were happy to print and broadcast this justification and to accept it at face value. Meanwhile, and notoriously, the City Council and the Mayor have long exempted from regulation two of the country's most notoriously polluting coal-fired plants, located in this same neighborhood. The two-decade struggle against these plants has shown that most Aldermen, city officials and state representatives have done little to back up their political claims of concern for the environmental health of Pilsen.

condition and not worth remodeling; the parents however understood La Casita as vital to their ability to care for their children as well as to their organizing efforts for better and more just access to education. A demolition order was issued. Parents were denied meetings with the Board of Education and with the elected officials responsible for allocating renovation funds. When police came to lock the building and post an eviction notice on the door, mothers and children occupied La Casita, demanding that the building be converted into a much-needed library instead.

The forty-three-day occupation was all over local and national news, from Fox News to the *Wall Street Journal* and the *Nation*, although poorly contextualized and often misrepresented. It was also sensationalized: mothers scuffling with cops, children blockading a school board meeting, community reactions when gas was cut off leaving parents and children with no heat in fifteen-degree weather, a demolition crew's refusal to carry out their survey ("We don't cross no picket lines," one of the guys proudly told moms). In general, the mainstream media represented the mothers as irrational, unreasonable and misinformed. The mostly immigrant, uneducated, middle-aged Latina mothers, many of whom are not native English speakers, many of whom are single mothers, were portrayed as being unwilling to grasp the inevitability and *reasonableness* of austerity cuts in times of financial crisis.

However, this same group of women had helped to uncover the scandal of divestment and theft of public funds, particularly TIF funds, in the city of Chicago, and called out their local officials on the systematic and racialized divestment of their neighborhood and their school. They exposed how the privatization of public schools is happening through the collusion of powerful private interests and local government, from the politically appointed Board of Education to elected officials such as ward Aldermen.[2] These moms are seasoned fighters who know, in specific and detailed terms, how public funds become private interest while low-income neighborhoods like theirs are starved of the most

2. In 1995, the Chicago public school system was put under mayoral control by former mayor Richard Daley. Among other implications, this has meant that the Board of Education is no longer an elected body. It is now appointed directly by the Mayor, run by a CEO and unaccountable to any public institution or forum. This model has become a blueprint for mayoral takeover of public school systems around the country. Chicago is divided into fifty legislative districts or wards. Each ward is represented by an elected Alderman; collectively, the fifty Aldermen form the City Council, the legislative body of the city government.

basic resources. This knowledge and experience of struggle manifested in the moms' refusal to acknowledge the legitimacy of the authority that the police or the Board of Education claimed to have over them. In the first solidarity statement, co-written with the moms on the second day of the occupation, we denounced the attack on La Casita as part of the wholesale privatization of public education in this country, which at the time we called an "extreme make-over" of the public sector. The statement was an attempt by people involved in solidarity organizing, such as myself, to contextualize this struggle and provide a counter-narrative to the mainstream media story: "The fight over the survival of this little field house is an important one in the larger struggles around educational rights, community self-determination and control over public land and institutions."[3]

At first, police attempted a forced eviction. Mothers and children responded by running into the building and locking themselves inside for several days. Arrest notices, trespassing notices, and threats of prosecuting parents for child endangerment were issued. Then, the occupation settled into a strange routine: children went to school during the day, allies came to provide around-the-clock support, especially during night "security shifts," and the blocks around the school were organized into an emergency phone tree. Between the field house and the school lies a playground where kids played and let off some steam during afternoon hours. Parents decided on clearing the playground in the morning, during school recess and when children left school at the end of the day, so that families who were not participating in the occupation, and who at times knew nothing of what was going on, would not be affected. Gradually, the group started organizing "shifts": parents and kids took turns sleeping in the field house overnight, about a third of the group at a time, to maintain the continuity of the occupation while offering a bit of much-needed relief to exhausted families. Some parents started sending their kids home at night while they themselves remained at La Casita. But sleep was minimal in the crowded building. Added to the stresses of the occupation itself, the moms were under the pressures of domestic expectations, caught in an irreconcilable conflict between their role in traditional patriarchal family arrangements in private home space and their role in a self-organized struggle against top-down political control over their communal home.

---

3. A petition and statement of solidarity with the Whittier parents, written on September 15, 2010, is available here: http://commonplacesproject.org/blog/?p=158.

Dozens, at times hundreds, of allies worked with parents to organize the best support they could: food, nighttime security shifts, media support, tactical and outreach support, cleaning, childcare. In an attempt to normalize life under always-changing conditions, parents collectively worked out schedules for eating, sleeping, cooking, cleaning, homework, and playtime as well as press conferences, strategy meetings, civil disobedience teach-ins, legal clinics, marches, and militant research. After the occupation, moms tried to return to "normal" in their domestic lives, but the transition has been a rocky one. The disruption of domestic relations has remained a private matter; although moms continue to give each other support, home life stays at home and has not yet been taken on as part of the collective struggle.

I became involved in ally organizing from the second day of the occupation. I spent most of my days at La Casita with my two-year-old daughter, enjoying the playground, sharing food and mingling with other toddlers, talking with moms, writing, discussing, sleeping, and then more playing and story-times. This has been my daughter's first experience of a school grounds, of struggle, and of communal living.

La Casita has two rooms: the front room was more public, serving as the logistics and meeting headquarters, dining hall, and media center. That's where hundreds of people who gathered to show support would enter in search of a bathroom or to offer some assistance, often unaware that the presence of so many new people—vastly outnumbering the parents—could become confusing and exhausting for parents and children. The back room became the children's play space and sleeping quarters, the more quiet space where moms would practice their speeches before a press conference, or fall apart, or comfort each other, where little ones napped, where story time happened. Here, a few allies would offer to care for kids while moms were in meetings and older siblings at school. After news reports that the occupation was partly a struggle for a school library, books started to come in—at first, from neighbors, but soon there were boxes and boxes from both local organizations and all over the country. Parents, children and a few allies found ourselves setting up makeshift shelves and crates, inventing a sorting system, and starting an inventory. Soon more books came; there were books everywhere and children using them. We reached out to the Chicago Underground Library, a group of activist-librarians who helped us develop and implement an unconventional cataloging and classification system. Within a few weeks, there were around 2,000 books shelved and organized, special collections, art supplies, and a check-in and check-out system. Inside a condemned building, a community and a library came to life.

Daniela and Maria, both Whittier students aged ten, became two of the main librarians. They learned the check-in system and set of categories for shelving; they read to younger kids and initiated the first public reading event of short essays written by themselves and their friends. They ran training sessions on the use of the library for their mothers, and were often in charge of a dozen or more younger children in the library. They taught everyone they could how to run the card catalog, how to check books in and out for themselves. They taught everyone, including other children as young as eight, how to be librarians like themselves. Daniela and Maria were best friends; during the occupation their moms became best friends and "sleeping buddies," coordinating their schedules so they would take overnight shifts at La Casita at the same time.

By the end of March, a few months after the occupation, my daughter and I were still going to the library. By then, it had over 5,000 books, including a social justice collection for kids and a Spanish and bilingual Spanish-English section. It is still kept alive by two of the moms, several allies and a core group of children. Spend an hour here, or just shuffle through the card catalog and look at the dozens of different children's handwriting and you'll realize: children are checking books out by themselves and for each other, they are doing inventory, re-shelving, and shaping the space according to their needs.

I sat down to talk with Maria and Daniela, as we do twice a week in our poetry workshop. Partway through the conversation, we were joined by another Whittier student, nine-year-old Dulce, a regular in the library. While Maria, Daniela and their moms were deeply involved in the struggle, Dulce's parents stayed out of the conflict and did not participate in the occupation. Consequently, Dulce saw many people she had never met before, but did not know what was happening. Most children attending Whittier Elementary School were in the same situation. By the time we recorded this conversation, the building had been saved, but the Board of Education has declared it unsafe for children while also withholding the funds promised for renovation. Fewer children are coming in as the struggle is now played out at weekly school board meetings downtown. I asked Maria and Daniela about their experiences and perspectives during this time. They both recounted the days of lock-down as terrifying: Daniela was locked in; Maria and her mom were locked out. That's when they became like sisters: they climbed on chairs to reach the high window on either side of the wall to talk and hold each other's hand.

Maria: When CPS (Chicago Public Schools) came, I saw these kids locked in. I saw Daniela and she looked like she was in jail. I felt guilty. What if something happened?

Daniela: Police came, and CPS, they began pushing people, and everyone was yelling. The alderman came with his people, and we knew he was against us. There were also many cameras, all the adults were yelling, the politicos were yelling at Evelyn, and she is like an aunt to me.[4]

Maria: At first I saw it on TV. I saw the police were here and kids were locked in, so I came to see with my mom. People were freaking out. There was a lock on the door and police cars everywhere. I was scared the building would be demolished with people inside it.

Did you understand what was happening? Who did you ask? Who talked to you?

Daniela: My mom explained that they were going to demolish the building. After the police left, she explained to me what happened, that they were fighting for a library and not to have the building demolished.

You knew there were signs posted on the door that said people would be arrested, that it was illegal to be in here?

Daniela: Yes. When I was locked in, I thought, "What am I doing here?" I thought, "What if something happens? What should I do?" My mom taught me to stick with Gema.[5] They would never arrest Gema because she is strong and she can fight them. Then she taught me how we were protesting and organizing. Protesting helped because it made me feel powerful.

---

4. The children and parents refer to the political class as "the politicos" or "the politics." They include elected officials and their wealthy campaign contributors, bureaucrats from city government and lawyers working on behalf of the city, political appointees, mainstream media reporters, and powerful local "well-meaning" religious and civil leaders who they see as being aligned with the power and interests of the political class. This does not automatically include police or crews contracted by the city, such as the demolition crew sent against them.

5. Gema Gaete and Evelyn Santos are two of the main, longstanding organizers involved with the Whittier Parent Committee.

Maria: Cheli (D's mom) became like my second mom. At first we didn't know what was happening, just that people were locked in, but Cheli always explained to us.

Daniela: It was very noisy. We were here with so many people and kids. I didn't know them very well, I didn't have a friend I knew or could rely on. Evelyn would say, "Let's color, kids," and try to do activities with us; Evelyn would try to entertain kids. My mom was panicking.

Maria: Yes, my mom too. Then she and Daniela's mom became best friends. Daniela would cry . . .

Daniela: I'd talk to Maria, sometimes only with Maria and not with my mom, because I didn't want to worry her. They were not getting any sleep.

There were many people here. How did you figure out who they were? I remember it was very confusing.

Maria: When Alvarez came, he started yelling at the kids.[6] Every time a politico came here, they had cameras and they would yell at the kids. Alvarez asked, "What does worthless mean?" and then he said we were wrong. He yelled at the kids in front of the cameras. But I stood up to him and said we need a library, that we don't have a library in the school and we deserve one.

Daniela: One day I was playing in the swings and a strange man came to take pictures. I ran to tell my mom because I thought he looked

---

6. Jose Alvarez was the chief of staff to former CPS CEO Arne Duncan. Alvarez is currently director of operations of CPS "New Schools" unit, i.e., the man in charge of tearing down existing facilities to make way for privatized schools. Arne Duncan is the current Education Secretary of the Obama administration, who is bringing the Chicago model of privatizing public schools—which begins with mayoral control and proceeds into the creation of a "public school market"—into national policy. This new model is backed by the largest education "stimulus" budget in the history of the country. The pace and aggression of this top-down remaking of public education is breathtaking and arguably unprecedented—and Alvarez, whom these girls confronted repeatedly, is one of its chief architects. During the occupation the girls and their mothers also confronted Alderman Danny Solis, several state representatives and Rahm Emanuel who passed through their neighborhood on his "listening tour" campaign. Emanuel had just resigned as Obama's chief of staff to begin campaigning for Mayor of Chicago.

suspicious and didn't know what he wanted. There were lots of people who were against us. Sometimes there were so many people, so much tension, and I felt they were putting everything on me.

Maria: The allies gave us a lot of support, bringing food and reading with us. I really liked meeting new people, sharing stories with outsiders and making great friends with the librarians, you and Robin and Lisa.[7] People stayed all night outside to do security. And people were sending books from Iowa and California. We helped clean the books and it was fun. I learned a lesson that you have to fight to get what you want.

What do you mean?

Daniela: Moms know they can do something. My mom looks big and bad but inside she was insecure. Now La Casita made her powerful. I used to put myself down, but now I think, "Who cares what other people think?" I learned to stand up.

Maria: Yes, we came here after school. My mom got involved because my sister and brother are now in college, but they came to school here, and she used to bring me here when I was little. Kids always stayed here to wait for parents or the older kids. The other parents and kids had stories of what I was doing here when I was little. It is like our home. When they said they would demolish it, it was like if your house was burned down, it was like a family member.

Daniela: During the sit-in this became my second home, even though we didn't have a past with it. But we stayed here, sleeping, eating. It's the best thing I ever did. I think it inspired people that they can't stop them, they can't take something you love away from you. It is amazing.

What about coming here after the sit-in?

Maria: Our library is really small. People are nice and you know everyone. They help us and we feel safe. After school I just come down

---

7. Robin Hewlett and Lisa Matuska are part of the large volunteer crew that helped build the library. They continue to conduct a weekly peace circle at La Casita, introducing Transformative Justice models to the struggle.

the stairs and come in here. And these books are special, they mean something more, they show that other people care and think about us.

Daniela: Yes, they have love. They have been given to us for what we are doing, not for pay. At the public library, it is different. They were friendly when my mom was there, but then they ignored me when she was away. There was a man in a rich suit whom the librarians helped and they ignored me. Here, no one thinks anyone is lower or higher.

Maria: Yes. Here we can come by ourselves and do things. We don't need adults to use the library.

What would you like to see different?

Maria: I think it needs to be organized more. Clean more, it's a bit dusty. We should make programs, not enough kids are coming

Daniela: Yes, no one has asked us to recruit more kids. The after-school programs visit each class and announce what is happening, but La Casita doesn't do this. Why are they not going class to class? Why are they not working with the school and the head of afterschool programs?

Maria: I told other kids to come, but if I tell Dulce to come here, her mom will say, "Who told you that?" It should come from an adult. If I was a parent, I would want adults to talk to my kid.

Dulce: I wasn't here during the sit-in. We didn't know something was going on. One day friends told me about the library, they said to come with them to get books. They were scared of new people. The day after, I started getting new books.

You didn't know anything was going on during the occupation?

Dulce: When the police were here, I came with my grandma, but no one explained so we just played in the playground. Sometimes the teachers used to ask questions.

What do you like about the library? Why do you come here every day?

Dulce: I think people come here for books and they learn to like reading. People that I know come. I don't know people in the big library, they are strangers. And it is easy [to get to La Casita]. You don't have to go on a train or a bus.

Daniela: People used to say, Why not give it up? But then the library started, and it was awesome! The same people who said that before, the teenagers, now started coming here.

Seven lessons on being an ally to parents and children during an occupation:

Based on our experiences, the small group of allies that was formed around the library collectively drafted a solidarity philosophy. I found this collective process of reflection and articulation to be personally very helpful. It led me to develop my own list of lessons, which reflect the mistakes I have made, the guidance I received from the parents, children, and allies I was closest to, and the specific ways in which I myself was able to participate in the struggle. Most of all, they reflect the mistakes I have made. These are lessons I offer myself, reminders, and bits of understanding I hope I can build upon and practice. I also offer these thoughts to whoever finds them useful or relevant to their own experience.

1. Solidarity has to do with being recognized in the eyes of another as an ally, based on one's actions. It has different and specific forms in each situation. Do not assume anything; learn it from the ground up.
2. Always introduce yourself—repeatedly. There can be a lot of confusion and parents are more likely to not express their anxieties in an effort to make children feel safe. There is a delicate balance between the need for help and the exhaustion and stress of dealing with many new people.
3. Learn names, especially the children's, and learn who is whose child. An occupation is a communal situation, where the nuclear family dissipates into a more open kinship structure. But this is temporary, and precarious. The need for security and familiarity may be heightened with exhaustion for both parents and children. Although sometimes all adults care for all kids and kids care for each other, parents and children may need to find each other in

a split second. You can help by keeping a watchful eye and a mental map of who is where at what time—you can help direct a confused child to their parent, or a worried mother to her child.

4. Help with the basics: cleaning, food, basic supplies, a small pot of flowers, those things that go unnoticed when present but are missed when neglected. Do not expect anything in return. Learn to cherish the thankless tasks.

5. An occupation will attract press in competition with each other. They will look for and focus on white Anglo subjects for the authoritative soundbite. Even if you speak to them and qualify your statements ("I am just an ally, I am only here to help," etc.), this will most likely be cut and your statements will be used to frame a representation of the struggle. Keep quiet; direct press to parents. If you see any press speaking with children without parents present, interrupt right away. Limit cameras around children.

6. When children are involved in an occupation, it is their struggle too. Learning how to be an ally to children is difficult. Parents will take on different roles; while some deal more with press, others may become logistics coordinators, while others may organize the basics of childcare. Some parents may become the main nodes to connect and include the children, not just as children but as participants with agency and stakes in the struggle. Find those parents. They will teach you.

7. When the occupation is over, everyone leaves. There may be no concrete tasks to accomplish, no obvious need for your presence. Stick around, come back to visit, spend time doing nothing, wait, be a friend, hang out. Returning to "normal" life is difficult and the needs of parents and children at this stage may be less clear. Occupation can be life-changing, but the full implications of these changes, and the ability to integrate them, may be slow to unfold. Solidarity has to do with being recognized in the eyes of another as an ally, based on one's actions. It has different and specific forms in each situation. Do not assume anything; learn it from the ground up.

New Kids on the Block
Ramsey Beyer

The one babysitting experience I ever had growing up was an awful one. Although most of my friends earned their money throughout high school by babysitting, it was never something that appealed to me. I didn't have younger siblings or relatives and had never had any experiences with small children. Children always seemed so fragile, and I was afraid that I would do or say something wrong.

Regardless, when I was sixteen, I reluctantly accepted my neighbor's plea to be her morning babysitter, just for an hour and a half, during the small overlap when she had to be at work early, before her husband got home from his night shift. They lived right across the street and I figured it was the least I could do to help her out since she had just started her own business and was probably very stressed. I arrived at 7 a.m., the kids were still sleeping, and I was hoping I could just ride it out that way until their father arrived. Unfortunately, that didn't happen. The youngest child, a two-year-old, awoke and began crying, and crying, and crying . . . and crying. I tried everything I could think of to calm him down, but finally buckled and called the mother at work. Oops, she had forgotten to tell me that her son was very sick and neglected to tell me about the medication I should give him. So I fumbled around with a sick crying baby and his medicine, trying to get him to take it, all while swearing off children for life. It was not the greatest first interaction with kids . . .

For years to come, I turned down babysitting offers and accepted my fate as a non-caregiver. Oddly enough, it wasn't until I moved away from my small town in Michigan to Baltimore that I started taking an interest in kids. To say I had culture shock would be an understatement. I had lived an insular white, rural, middle class life. Most of my experiences were with my own family and my small circle of friends at my small school. In the city, people interact—at least in Baltimore they do. You can't walk down the street without some form of interaction with mere strangers. Needless to say, urban life is very different from the life I had growing up. I was surprised to see young kids playing by themselves on the sidewalk in the city I had been warned about for crime and violence.

By the time I graduated from college and moved off campus, I was used to brief interactions with people of all ages. Kids were especially forward. I moved into a family neighborhood, surprisingly mixed in class and race. I was no longer in my mostly white, art school neighborhood. In Baltimore, I noticed many households where grandmothers, mothers, and children all lived together with no fathers present. Up and down our block were families like these with young kids, mostly under ten years old. It was inevitable that I was going to get to know these families in one way or another, and, as a household of slightly punk-looking, twenty-something white kids, we were determined to make sure our neighbors, none of whom were white, felt comfortable with our presence. The easiest way to do this was through the kids on the block. They were already curious about us and introduced themselves right away. The kids immediately surrounding our house, from several families, were all five and six years old, and had personality! We couldn't ignore them if we had wanted to (not that we did want to). Whenever we sat on our front porch, we were inundated with questions from the kids next door. They were especially interested in the fact that we rode bicycles to get around, instead of taking cars, and they loved to show off their bike skills, especially wheelies and no-handers. At first, our interactions were mostly limited to the kids shouting, "Hey! Watch this!" and we'd politely watch, and usually give them exaggerated gasps to show them how impressed we were.

At first, their parents would yell at them for "bothering us" and warn them about pestering adults. We would politely smile and go inside. It was not our place to contradict any parents and we were especially cautious of the kids viewing us as "the good guys" because we never had to tell them what to do or reprimand them as their parents would occasionally have to. Over time, we hung out on our porches more often, usually playing guitar, fixing our bikes, reading or drawing, and we were always a magnet for the kids on the block. The kids asked surprisingly inspired questions and made curious observations about our hobbies, very different from those of their own families. It was then that I realized that to relate to kids, all I had to do was give them credit for their own intelligence. I didn't need to talk to them any differently, act in a special way, or do things differently than I normally would. I could just "hang out" with them and they'd be happy about it. Though their parents didn't always understand that we didn't mind hanging out with the kids, they eventually began to trust us.

From time to time, the kids would want to play outside longer than their parents wanted. A common rule on the block was that the kids could only play if an adult was watching. As parents wanted to go inside and told their kids that "time was up," the kids began pleading, "Look, they're still outside!" and we would confirm that we planned to stay outside and didn't mind watching over the kids. As non-parents, non-"real world" adults, we found an important role for ourselves. We weren't constantly around the kids. We weren't working to feed them. We weren't tired. We could just be there, and in a way, give a break to the parents that always had to be there and had to work very hard for their kids.

We began assuming this role more vigorously. We would come outside specifically to hang out with the kids. We'd often bring activities outside, allow kids to ride on our skateboard, play our guitars, draw with our crayons, and show off how well they could write their own name. As time went on, we even had a mini-fundraiser to get a kids' basketball hoop that we locked to our front porch. Until then, the kids would just dribble and fake shoot. They loved the hoop and it certainly opened a can of worms. We had to be constant referees and even had to take the hoop down when we couldn't monitor it. Eventually, the hoop broke from too much activity and big kids from other blocks coming to play on it.

When summer came around, there was an initiative from the neighborhood association called the "Porch Book Reading Project" and we instantly decided to participate. We set up our porch as a "reading porch" one hour, one day a week. We put up a banner when it was reading time, brought out a big basket of books on all topics, and sat with the kids encouraging them to read and talk about what they had read. The project was set up to keep kids reading over the summer. The kids were surprisingly enthusiastic for a chance to show off what they had been learning during the school year, and, as non-parents, we were able to show our genuine enthusiasm because we didn't have to work with them on it all the time. Some kids would come just for a snack; others were actually excited to read. Regardless, they kept coming back until we were too busy to keep up with the reading day.

At this point, parents on the block completely trusted us with their kids and we had cordial relationships with the parents as well, something that easily might not have happened if we didn't bother to befriend their children. Unlike other kids in the neighborhood, the neighbors' kids weren't allowed to leave the block. However, because we were willing to spend some time with them, the parents allowed them to leave the block if they were accompanied by one of us. We'd gladly walk them over to get "snowballs," or ride bikes with them around the block, and often would invite them in on nights when we had acoustic musicians play in our living room. As a "punk house" that had constant activity, it was especially mind-boggling for these young urban kids as well as for the bands passing through. Many bands from across the country commented on how exciting it was to see our interactions with the people in our neighborhood and how much fun it was to have the kids come inside to listen to music and play on their drums.

Our strangeness to the kids was apparent. Many of the boys were blown away that I could fix their bike and that I had muscles. They said girls weren't supposed to have muscles. When it was time for a new roommate to move into our house, one of the kids asked if we would ever have a black roommate. I assured him that we definitely would if we had things in common. When we were looking for a roommate, we wanted someone who liked bikes, similar music, etc. This was very interesting to them. One morning, another kid said he had hot dogs for breakfast and asked if I liked hot dogs. I told him I don't eat meat. He asked why not and I responded with "I don't know, I just don't like to." We were always cautious to not step on the toes of the kids' parents, bringing up some sort of conflicting views. The little boy responded by saying, "I think it's sad that some meat comes from animals. Our meat doesn't though. It comes from Giant." (Giant is the local grocery store chain.) They were always blowing us away with funny insights like this. Later, another little boy asked about gay people. The kids would tiptoe over and say, very shyly, "Ramsey? Um . . . I have a question . . ." and would propose some question that they thought we might have an answer to that they hadn't heard from their parents.

As non-parents, we could offer second-hand advice, about school, bullies, friends, and we did, often. The kids relied on us for an outside perspective. In return, they gave us the chance to think about our own opinions and how and why they might differ from those of an urban black family. Self-awareness is an easy thing to lose when you keep yourself in a homogeneous community.

In the end, I think I learned more in my year and a half after college, just living in Baltimore, than I did in my entire four years at school. Thanks to the kids, I had a lot more fun too.

Lactivists Do It Better: What Radical Parents' Allies Can Learn from La Leche League International
Mariah Boone

Sitting in a session on effective writing at a regional La Leche League International conference, I can hear a toddler crying through the walls. The sounds of children are everywhere in this hotel, but I become increasingly uncomfortable with this particular sound, my tingling breasts clueing me into the possibility that this is my own toddler. I slip out the door and head towards the children's craft room. Before I get there, I see a mother who lives in a city about two and a half hours north of my own coming out of the craft room.

"Is that Marigold?" I ask.

"Yeah," she replies. "I think she's having a little meltdown."

The craft room isn't really a babysitting gig—just a children's space. Children are welcome in every part of the conference, so babysitting isn't much of an issue. That said, kids can get bored with forums and workshops after a while, so there are craft and activity rooms set up where parents or family members or allies can take them for some kid-focused fun in the midst of all the serious session offerings. Volunteers help in these areas with craft and game ideas. I find my two-year-old, comfort her, and return to my session, leaving her happily constructing a shaking instrument out of an old plastic juice jug, straws, beads, and dowel pieces. At a conference that covers such diverse topics as political advocacy, contraception, special needs infants, legal issues surrounding breastfeeding, breastfeeding and HIV, and loving discipline, we close with a performance scripted and choreographed by the older children who are attending. The kids sing and dance a song about the sea with ocean-themed cut-outs they have made to celebrate our coastal city where the conference took place, drawing in families from all over our state and beyond. Everyone loves it.

At other La Leche League International events, such as annual World Walk for Breastfeeding marches and baby fairs held to raise awareness, my experiences have been similar. Just as everyone expects mothers to include their children and take care of their children's needs at La Leche League meetings, La Leche League advocacy and awareness raising actions are planned with the assumption that children will be an integral part of everything. That's the way League mamas do it.

As a single, childless activist in my college days, I don't remember seeing very many children at the demonstrations and speaking events that I organized and in which I participated. The same was true of all the block walking and phone banking I did in political campaigns at the time. I was mostly surrounded by my own kind, and my own kind was a bunch of college kids who had not had any truck with family responsibility. It wasn't really on our radar yet.

Certainly there were exceptions. There was the mother of two little girls who helped out in the 1992 Clinton campaign. She was always either leaving them somewhere else or bringing them along to the county headquarters. In my ignorance, I felt sorry for them and thought she should be more focused on their needs, as if public policy did not directly impact the meeting of their needs. There was also a peace activist in my college town who involved her children in everything and actually planned one action that I remember that included the children of the community. Knowing her, I started to feel just an early glimmer that children could and should be involved in activism, but most of the people around me felt differently and were very critical of her parenting. Outside of those two families, I did not see children involved in the rather wide range of events that comprised my college activism, and I never felt like it was my responsibility to support those mothers and their children as part of our work for social change.

Fortunately, La Leche League International was there to show me a different way when my first child came along.

I always knew that I would nurse my children. Giving them the gift of my milk and all that it could do for them was a huge priority for me. As a working mother, however, I needed some help to be successful at pumping and managing the very difficult balancing act of being employed outside the home while nursing an infant. I started attending La Leche League meetings when I was pregnant and found a support group that kept me sane through the years when my responsibilities were pretty overwhelming.

La Leche League International is based on a mother-to-mother support model—mothers help other mothers get the information and support they need to breastfeed. The organization was sparked because of a conversation at a picnic in 1956 when two nursing mothers began talking about the lost art of breastfeeding. The two mothers kept talking and soon seven mothers were talking. By inviting other nursing mothers to talk about breastfeeding, they began a support network that now includes 3,000 meetings in 66 countries. Today, LLLI serves as a consultant to UNICEF, the World Health Organization, and other international policymaking bodies, although only thirty employees staff the entire organization. The majority of its work is still done, all over the world, by volunteer mothers with children in tow.

Children are always present at League events. Their needs are not only tolerated and planned for; they are celebrated. Complicated advocacy work involving public health and human rights takes place side by side with crafts and stories. No one takes any activist less seriously because she has a child in her lap at a La Leche League conference and there are always willing arms to pass children among whenever they are needed. Marches and events are planned under the assumption that children of various ages will be involved and that all activities take into account the needs of mothers and children—time and place and safety needs as well as developmental and even recreational needs. Marching routes are short enough for fresh-out-of-the-stroller preschoolers to manage, and marches are even held indoors if outdoor weather is hazardous. Crafts, games, and storytelling take place alongside the serious advocacy work at League events and some sessions are planned specifically for children, such as yoga and healthy cooking classes. At League events, everyone expects to hear the happy and not-so-happy sounds of children everywhere. People know mothers will be changing diapers and nursing children as they work. Everyone is willing to a hold a willing baby or entertain a fractious child. This is part of the work—possibly the most important part.

The work of La Leche League grew around kitchen and coffee tables and always took into account the busy lives of mothers. Every mother's contribution was valued and the work was parceled out among many so that everyone could make a contribution. As the organization has grown, that mother-friendly style of activism has continued. As a La Leche League editor once put it to me to assure me that she was not worried that my employment and family responsibilities would interfere with an assignment we were discussing: "These are mother-sized volunteer jobs."

Having experienced the mother-friendly style of lactivism that I found in my years as a member of La Leche League International, I have always known that my children belong in my public life, not closed away from it. They are citizens of the world, just as I am, and they must know the world to live in it wisely. I do not believe in closing them up in a pretty children's ghetto where they cannot act to shape their own futures or that of their world. My children have attended many demonstrations and other actions with me as we together work to make the world a better place. I am the mother at the Commission on Children and Youth meeting with the crayons and the glue sticks. I am the one at the peace march with the stroller. There are kids holding signs with me to protest war toys outside the Wal-Mart on Black Friday, and that was my twelve-year-old phone banking for the Obama campaign. Usually, my kids are the only kids there, but we keep coming.

I know from remembering my own strange judgmental thoughts from the days when I was a childless activist that people are not always looking at our little family with kindness at the rallies, marches, and meetings at which we are so visible. I also know, however, that they will never see another way if they do not actually see another way, so I will keep showing them our way and hope that it grows on them.

La Leche League International showed me that children belong in my world, that they are full citizens and should not be excluded from public life. I learned that any important work can be done with children around if the work is spread out reasonably and planned with the needs of families always in mind. I learned that activists can support each other and that there are enough arms if the arms are willing. I also learned that children make everything more beautiful and full of joy, if also more sticky and, well, loud. Activists in all change movements should know that they need the viewpoints and contributions of parents to reach their goals, and that parents need support in order to contribute as much as they can. Activists who wish to help the parents in their movements to contribute can learn the lessons that I learned as a lactivist. Allies can be those willing arms.

The Unfinished Universe
Darran White Tilghman

As a kid, it was hard to explain what my parents' business, the Unfinished Universe, was. It is maybe even harder now. It was a furniture restoration and woodworking shop they started with their best friend in the 1970s in Lexington, Kentucky. It was part artists' colony, part revolutionary business, part rehab center, part college dorm. It was the name of the book that, even then, my dad sensed he would never finish writing. It was the kind of place people liked to just come and be. Growing up there, being welcomed as a kid there, formed my worldview and certainly my ideas about what a workplace can and should be.

In the 1960s, at the University of Kentucky (UK)'s English department, my dad taught classes on Western Lit and the counterculture (but everyone just called them Pat White's classes). He was an excellent teacher. In 1972, after the shootings of students at Kent State, UK students were staging sit-ins in protest. After getting a phone call from a parent asking him to check up on her daughter, he joined his students, sat with them, as he loved to do. He never was radical, but he didn't like to be told what to do. When the campus cops told him he couldn't cross a police line to help an older visiting professor who found himself in the fray and was being treated roughly, my dad simply said, "I'm crossing the line." And so he was tear-gassed, arrested, and denied tenure, probably to the relief of the administration.

When he left the university, he and Joel Evans started polishing hardware. Joel was a physics PhD student, pissed off at UK and cut loose by them, too. Someone called Joel the smartest redneck you'll ever meet, and he is equally crass and brilliant. I've seen him in furious, drunken, foul-mouthed arguments about opera singers. At some point in my childhood, I realized that whenever I pictured Santa Claus, or a vengeful God, I was thinking of Joel. Polishing hardware, if you like learning, can lead you to furniture repair, and repairing can lead you to designing and building and teaching. At least that's how I think the Unfinished Universe evolved. When I've asked my mom how she got involved in starting a business when she and my dad were not yet married, she replied, "Well, I had the money for the down-payment on the van." The shop just seemed like a good idea to the three of them.

There was no political agenda at the Unfinished Universe, or the UU as we called it. The unofficial slogan was "Slow, but Expensive," but the shop was never a great moneymaker. Instead it was honest and fair and hired all kinds of people (repeat offenders, single mothers, struggling musicians, dissatisfied lawyers), plenty of whom no one else would hire. By 1978, the shop was up and running (up and down and running), and the world had changed again, and my dad was sought out for an interview as an expert or at least a source on Revolution.

In 2010, two years after his death, I heard that interview for the first time. The sound (transferred from reel to cassette at some point, and now to disc) pops and hums with the past. I love listening to my dad (I always did), to the thoughtful way he would pause to ready an answer for you, for anyone, in his sweet deep voice. Where, the earnest interviewer wanted to know, did the Revolution go? Pat White could repeat a question in a way that made it sound almost rhetorical; there were people who thought he never meant to answer at all.

In the background of his long thoughtful pause after that question, I heard a time capsule of my childhood in the Unfinished Universe. Our family dogs crowding under the workbench, the lullaby noises of the drill presses and band saws, and my patient mother, who would have been eight months pregnant with me, talking to the customers, answering the phone, running the business of the business. Soon I would be born into that universe, and play in the wood shavings, and answer the phones, and learn to cut my own jigsaw puzzles. My dad's kids and Joel's kids grew up in the shop. My sister Sully was one of the great long-time employees. The UU didn't just let you bring your kids to work; it employed your kids, and your friends' kids, and your kids' friends.

A distillation, then, of ideas for welcoming kids in the workplace (and, I guess, the world):

- Include them. I always felt like I was helping and I was a part of things (though Joel would always say, "Goddammit, you missed all the good stuff!").
- Participate in your coworkers' parenting experience; innovate. Anyone in the shop might teach me how to change a saw blade

or cane a chair. I was once famously wrapped in T-shirts when the diaper bag had gone with my mother on delivery in the shop van. Everyone pitched in.

• Allow children to experience. When I was learning to turn wood on the lathe, a fairly dangerous and usually masculine craft, Joel would make special gouges, the chisel-like tools used in turning, for my small hands. Turning wood on a lathe has some aspects in common with throwing clay on a wheel, the sensuous sculpting symmetry of it, but the early stages are a lot like sticking a screwdriver into a fan. As I stood by the spinning block of wood, all centrifugal force (another concept Joel taught me), no one watched over me. But Joel would stop by once in a while. "Looks good, Sweetheart," he'd say. "You're gettin' good shavings. *If ya fuck up, don't worry about it.*"

And so I grew up, with all my fingers and a feeling of being part of something, knowing what it is to fuck up and still to like work. I moved to Baltimore and came to work as the Director of Development at the Village Learning Place, or VLP, a weird and wonderful community library and learning center in Charles Village. The VLP is another place I have difficulty describing, even though it has essentially been my job to do just that for the past four years. Through free programs and library resources, the VLP works to support kids and families. It is also an incredibly family-friendly workplace as well as its own motley grassroots movement. In my five years there, four of my coworkers and I brought our babies to work with us, shared in raising them, and continue to be rewarded by the connections between parenting and the mission and work of a good nonprofit.

At an all-staff meeting at the VLP in my eighth month of pregnancy, my soon-to-be Sukie was doing that variety of fetal movement that simultaneously brings to mind a porpoise (full, rolling dives) and an escape artist (straitjacket). As I shifted under the turbulent swell, first one and then all of my coworkers stopped to marvel just for a moment at the small spectacle of it. Look at that *baby*! And instead of politely ignoring me, they participated with me, and let me experience something I didn't want to miss. It was an interruption of maybe ten seconds that deepened my respect for my coworkers and my joy in my life and work.

Ideas on how to welcome parents and their profound little interruptions in the workplace:

- Build policies and procedures that support parenting: maternity/paternity leaves, flexible schedules, working from home. Talk about options. Acknowledge the humanness of families.
- Rethink "professional." Whenever possible, be understanding about babies giggling at meetings, grown-ups whispering during naptime, a sign on the door that says, "Pumping: out soon!"
- Welcome kids' stuff (portable crib, play mat, bouncy seat) to live in shared space.
- Appreciate that a parent in the workplace is simultaneously doing two full-time jobs, and inevitably sometimes fails at one or both of them, but ultimately can enrich both. (*If ya fuck up, don't worry about it.*)

"So where did it go?" the interviewer asks. "Where is it now?"

"Where did the Revolution go?" my father repeats, thirty-three years ago. Tape static and shop sounds as he pauses so characteristically. You can almost hear him look around at the sawdust and the dogs, the pregnant second wife, before he answers with a tone of self-evidence. "Places like this."

Three

WHAT'S GENDER, RACE, AND CLASS GOT TO DO WITH IT?

Maybe we poor welfare women will really liberate women in this country. We've already started on our own welfare plan. Along with other welfare recipients, we have organized so we can have some voice. Our group is called the National Welfare Rights Organization (N.W.R.O.). We put together our own welfare plan, called Guaranteed Adequate Income (G.A.I.), which would eliminate sexism from welfare. There would be no "categories"—men, women, children, single, married, kids, no kids—just poor people who need aid. You'd get paid according to need and family size only and that would be upped as the cost of living goes up. —Johnie Tillmon, "Welfare Is a Women's Issue," *Ms. Magazine* 1, no.1 (Spring 1972).

Mothers and fathers do not encounter the same struggles. Families of color are disproportionately vulnerable and subject to state violence, criminalization, separation from their families, and other systemic injustices. Power imbalances affect families—and the right to family—in many different ways. The rights of many individuals in different groups to have, keep, and raise their children are often under attack.

The news is filled with stories illustrating how the system reinforces race, class, and gender oppressions. As our book entered its final editing stages, Tanya McDowell, a homeless black mother in Connecticut, was arrested and sentenced to prison for trying to improve her child's education by enrolling him in a different school district. At the same time, Florida police refused to arrest George Zimmerman for over a month after he followed, shot, and killed seventeen-year-old Trayvon Martin simply because Trayvon was black and wearing a hoodie. We cannot talk about social justice without recognizing the intersections of race, class, gender, and other identities.

This Poem Is in Honor of Mothers

Tiny a.k.a. Lisa Gray-Garcia

Houseless mothers and
poor mothers
Low-wage mothers and
no-wage mothers
Welfare mothers
And three job working
mothers
Immigrant mothers
And incarcerated
mothers

In other words
This poem is in honor of
INS-ed with,
CPS-ed withed and
Most of all
System-messed with
mothers

This poem is in honor of all those
poor women and men
And yes
I said men
Cause don't sing me that old song
About gender again

Who fight and struggle
And steal and beg

In every crevasse
And corner
to keep their kids in a bed
Who dress and feed
with tired hands
Who answer cries
over and over again

This poem is in honor of all those
Mothers
who deserve to be coddled
And loved

Fed and protected
Instead of criminalized,
Marginalized
and rarely respected

Who can barely make it but always do
And still raise all the worlds' people
Like me
you
and you

Can I get a witness?

This poem is in honor of mothers

Who can barely make it
But sometimes do . . .
And still raise all the worlds' people
Like me
you
and you

Is Everyone at the Table? An Interview with Noemi Martinez, Fabiola Sandoval, and Maegan "la Mamita Mala" Ortiz — Three Single Mother of Color Media Makers

Victoria Law and China Martens

Questions: Could you tell us where you live and a little bit about yourself? What are your particular struggles as a single mother of color? Could you share some ideas/ tips on concrete ways to support radical single mothers of color and their children?

Noemi Martinez: I live in deep South Texas, ten minutes away from the Mexican border, the Rio Grande Valley. I'm a single mami to River, age ten, and Winter, age six. I write the zine *Hermana, Resist* as well as edit other zines, currently *Voices Against Violence* and *Finding Gloria: Nos/ Otras*, a vegan recipe zine called *Sofrito Pa' Ti*. I do community work involving survivors of violence, alternative media. I document stories, lives, and record our history.

I think the most important thing to understand is no one will know if someone needs help, or assistance, or is open to giving ideas on how to be more inclusive to kids and parents, or if your "solutions" are really helpful, if they don't engage in conversations with single mamis and make them part of the discussion, offering choices and understanding time restraints of a single mami. Also, it's very frustrating to be asked to spearhead the project of making a particular event or space kid-friendly to the mamis themselves. One of the problems single mamis have is never having the opportunity to relax and take part in discussions or meetings, classes or workshops. To put the mamis in charge of finding solutions and putting these options in place is not taking into consideration the challenges of a single mami. Asking single mamis to find solutions that organizations create, in creating spaces that are not parent or kid friendly is also inappropriate. Organizers and groups are in much better positions financially, often with unlimited supply of paid or volunteer hours (how many organizations have full-time/part-time organizers?) and have the connections to get volunteers to conduct questionnaires, conduct studies and develop different scenarios to solve the solutions of the problems within their own organization/group/ circle. For example, I really am not equipped to answer questions of finding concrete solutions to particular problems. I might be coming across as selfish, but I just don't have the patience and time for every step of how to make an event or workshop kid and single mami friendly. Asking the mamis just seems backwards to me.

• • •

Fabiola Sandoval: I live in South Los Angeles, California, with Amaya, my five-year-old daughter, my seven-pound dog Cafe and my cat Lucky. I work at a nonprofit in South Los Angeles where I wear many hats (too many at moments), co-chair a women's action coalition in downtown, when I do my own thing at work, don't eat right, or dig into my sleeping time. I blog at fabmexicana.com among other publications. I've written for *make/shift: feminisms in motion*, political zines and the downtown community paper, *The Community Connection*. The topics I've mostly written about are gentrification in the city, "mental health," stories and poems of my childhood and adult life. I write mostly on paper everyday and sometimes I feel like I drown in my own words before finding my way up to catch air and, on occasion, I meet the sacred via paper. Oh, and lately I've been getting lost in books.

I'm with my daughter half the time. I share custody with her father. A particular struggle I'm having as a single mother that's sharing custody with the father of my child is trying to figure out ways to navigate an often hostile situation. Speaking of writing, that's one piece of my life that needs a lot of documentation for sanity, to keep my story straight for record keeping and healing, that's a constant. This struggle in self-preservation and self-protection is an extra layer; I feel that I'm spreading myself thin due to time/energy is a constant state of being. It's very difficult. Though I am fortunate enough to have good friends and a job that's pretty flexible and supportive, the eight-hour plus full-load workday is difficult with the zigzagging in traffic, long commute, and feeling a scarcity of a proximity network of community is something very difficult on my own mental health, contributing to a feeling of isolation, the lack of creativity and time/energy for tangible community-building let alone writing/creating/photography.

To Organizations:

Make the environment child-friendly by saying it is and then acting on it by allowing children in the space, making it fun (as possible). Stay honest to your mission. Revisit it. Have community members on your boards and evaluate your impact on how you affect families in your communities, especially families that are the most marginalized in the neighborhoods you're in. Look at the income disparities, and class/race make up of things; see if you're emulating society in the way you deal with differences, cutbacks, and militancy of ideas. Of course we all do, but let's try and work to change it. Support the papas/mamas of your organization. As mamas, we can try to influence, if it's possible, by bringing our children to these places and making them family-friendly by our actions. Dreaming here, but if I can work a less than twenty-five hour workweek with benefits and decent living wage for everyone all over the world. Another world . . . yes, I know.

To Panels:

Saying it's okay if children make noise, that this is a family-friendly space by having a host of child-friendly activities available. As caretakers and caretaker allies, we can suggest that before the panel, while the panel is being planned, if possible. But the most ideal would be having childcare available, paying for the child to go to the conference too, and thinking about intergenerational spaces.

To Conferences:

Ditto to Noemi. Don't make parents do all the work. We work like everybody else and are raising children; that's hard in itself. A lot of us have soul-enriching passions such as writing and have other relationships to keep, plus we need to take care of ourselves by sleeping well, eating right, and moving our limbs other than our brains and fingers to keep healthy and raise healthy children. So let's spread the work to as many folks as possible. That would be the most sensitive thing to do.

To Exes:

Try, just try, to be harmonious and decent. Dissin' the baby mama is not fighting the power nor is it revolutionary. Out of love, I'm not trying to marginalize single papas of color. Reconciliation and self-love is the best that can be done for the children.

To Each Other:

Caretakers and non-caretakers, whether single/or not/with more than one child, we can do this. We can share with each other, lift each other up, and understand if someone needs more help, that's okay. If someone needs to back off for a bit to work on other things, that's okay. We lift each other up with words, deeds, or even just good thoughts. It's important to be critical, yes, always, critical relationships that lift. Everyone has traumas; sometimes that's hard. Listening is good, really good. Not trying to sound patronizing, but it's really great to ask a person how they are doing, what are they up to, how are their kids. To non-parents, remember we're raising children, it's a little different. Our time and energy is limited so keep that in mind when you're thinking about inviting us to commit to a project, an organization, or even your party and city. If so, support, support, support. All of us, parents and non-parents.

This world cannot eat us alive because we are sensitive, supportive, and loving to each other even if we have pretty differing perspectives and capacities. We will more than survive we will thrive. To support one another, engage politically, center personal and collective healing and a world that lifts children and creativity are values that I want to foster in anything I'm in.

To Ourselves:

Don't be too hard on yourself for not writing the book, the zine, or creating the community center or bomb-ass garden yet and blowing it up with projects. Love yourself, surround yourself with loves, feed that body healthily and move those limbs to some adrenaline-inducing activities *seguido* (constantly), everyone but especially people of color working to make change. We need to live long lives to see the changes of making our communities, orgs, each other more in line with values of reciprocity, dignity for everyone, caretaking the earth, the young and older ones and one that flourishes with creativity daily.

I keep dreaming and staying busy with actions, knowledge gaining, not trying to lose weight by poor eating habits, raising my daughter to be sensitive, caring, strong, think about the world, writing and loving.

• • •

Maegan a.k.a. la Mamita Mala: I live in Casa Mala in Corona, Queens, NYC, with my two ChileRican chicas: La MapucheRican, age twelve, and Miss Poroto, age three. I'm an espanglish poet, political blog-ger, freelance writer and mami'activista. I help run *VivirLatino*, a mujer-owned and run daily Latino politics and culture blog. This is my writing year so I am working on a poetry manuscript and a project documenting the place of radical women of color, mamis of color and people of color in general on the Internets.

My biggest struggle is with time and silence. My work requires time and attention, the same time and attention that my children require. I'm not a newbie at writing or as an activist but that doesn't mean I don't need help. It also shouldn't mean that my presence is unwelcome be-cause my presence comes with a child. It gets to the point that you start to internalize it. There are so many events, conferences, trainings that I wouldn't even bother to apply for because I start to stress about childcare and money. I have been invited to speak at events all around the country, including events being marketed to women, but have had to not attend because it's assumed that I have hundreds of dollars stashed away and can fly off on my own dime and be reimbursed later. This is called bullshit inclusion. Organizations claiming to represent the voice of women invite a woman of color and when she can't go they can sit back comfortably and say, "Well, we invited her." I see it also when working with other men of color. It's easier for orgs to deal with them because it's not as messy. As a single mami of color I will ask about childcare, I will ask for funding to speak. In this year I am recognizing that it's okay to ask for these things. My work/words are valuable. My mami'hood adds to that value. Recognize.

To Orgs:

If you invite me to an event and you know I am coming with child/children, make sure that all the attendees know that the event is child-friendly. I was invited to cover an immigration conference but had to bring my toddler. I left one meeting in tears because one conference at-tendee treated my daughter and me so poorly. I know many orgs are just starting to deal with mamis and kids in their spaces, so I am appreciative but still demanding :)

To Non-Mami Colleagues:

When something is being planned, ask if women/mamis of color are being included. If they are not, why? Is it because the space isn't ac-cessible? Ask us why we are not at the table!!!

How to Build a Community That Involves Single Parents
Noemi Martinez

- Consider your definition of community.
- Realize that people are parents. Realize that parents are people. Realize that parents are the same people you knew before.
- Realize that parents can be activists. But they are also parents. They have different things on their mind. Single parents often have things such as food, rent, money, health on their mind. Unlike the single person, they are usually thinking of their child(ren) when they think about these things. Sometimes a single parent like me cannot concentrate on the latest protest, important as it may be, because I may be thinking of what my next job will be, and the addition and subtraction of money in my head.
- **Realize the different situations of a single parent and a family that has two parents. If you don't realize the difference, start asking questions.**
- Don't roll your eyes when someone brings up childcare.
- Consider why your community involvement only concerns the childless or those that can leave their kids with someone else, the other parent, a spouse or a friend. (Yes, in theory, the children can be left with babysitters. Who need to be paid.)
- Think about why parents stop being involved in community events, conferences, trainings, meetings, and skillshares. If single parents don't feel that you or the community cares about what it means to be a parent, a single parent, they won't seek you out for help. It will not feel like a community; it will not feel like a welcoming community.
- Consider if you are secretly thankful that snotty, bratty kids are not around to ruin your utopian experience.
- Realize that parenting and being a role model to kids in your community are important because they will be the activists of tomorrow.
- Consider why access to cultural events, planning, and meetings for single

parents is not important enough for you to have considered before.
- Consider why motherhood and, heavens forbid, single parenthood are seen as a step back in the eyes of activists and feminists.
- Consider what it would mean for the next generation to care about the same things you care about. Consider when and how will this happen?
- **Realize that racism almost always comes into play for single mothers of color.**
- Consider what new skills and influences single parents can give their children, if the community thinks it's important for them to be involved.

These concerns may never be resolved, but it is crucial to consider some reasons why the single parents in your communities might not be receptive to your call for actions.

Mami vs. Mommy, Mami'hood vs. Motherhood: What Do Mami Movements Need?

Maegan "la Mamita Mala" Ortiz

I attended the Women's Equity Media Summit (WEMS) in Detroit. To say that it was an uncomfortable space would be too simple. There was a sense among many of the women of color I was with that we *had* to be there, since many of us had been given some money to help defray our travel costs. We would have been in Detroit anyway for the Allied Media Conference (AMC) and, truth be told, we weren't sure why we had been invited into the WEMS space. What was the mission and what was expected of us radical women of color media-makers?

We gathered in one corner of the room, close to the door, forming a protective circle of love and support around each other as other women spilled their female creds on the table, leaving many of us feeling marginalized. What of us who didn't claim the word woman or the word feminist? What made one a "woman" in that space? Was it being born with a white vagina? Did bringing up these issues make us automatic enemies of the space of chairs and tables that wound around the conference room? What of us who had no interest or desire to be part of a non-profit structure? What of us who didn't want their money?

The gathering of mamis emerged. That's right, mamis, not mommies. I even had to correct the spelling on the butcher paper at the front of the room, because for the last twelve years (*carajo* I feel *vieja*), it has been made clear to me that my experiences are not the ones being blogged about or written about in books. After all, it was my mami'hood, with all the sex/gender/race/class/language issues you can pull from that word, that started me seeking others like me through blogging and organizing on the ground. My use of the word "mami" is based in my Latina/WOC identity, in the hypersexualization or the diminishing of my sexuality. My mami'hood is a fucking community that I am working every damn moment to create and live; it is not a marketing tool or playdate.

As Noemi of *Hermana, Resist* says:

> I'm supposed to explain to someone who doesn't even get the difference between Mami and Mommy, I'm supposed to explain to them why my form of media is valid in their movement? I'm supposed to try to sell you on my career? What career? This is my life, my kids' life, our sanity. And for the record, no, we don't start our "media" after we get funded and no we don't start working on "media" when we're up for a sabbatical. No, we don't start any "movement" after our grant gets accepted. Some money might come along the way, someone will donate $10 or $50 or someone gets a scholarship to attend a conference that'll be critiqued the hell outa.

It gets tiring having to explain mami vs. mommy, mother, mom. I probably shouldn't frame it as a vs., cuz it's not like mommy media makers, mom 2.0ers and mamis are fighting each other. Most of the time, we're ignoring each other. I can't say exactly why the moms/mommies/mothers ignore radical mamis of color, especially us single media maker ones. After I explained "mami" to one woman at the conference, she walked away, giving the two other mamis and me her back. "Guess she's not a mami," one of us said shrugging.

One of the first exercises I did in my small caucus of three that included Brownfemipower and Noemi, was around what we need in order to do our work, which we translated to "what do mami movements need?" Here is a list of what I came up with:

mami'hood
justicia
not speaking for people
comunidad
multi-lengua'ed
access
accountability
amor
apoyo
collective
seguridad
multiple points/ways of entry
poesia
arte

sexo
child-inclusive
childcare
sustainability
flexibility

What does your list look like?

Pero when the applause and the patting on the back stops, when the one-on-one conversations in corners that amount to nothing but some white *mujer* telling us thanks for doing/saying the things I'm too lazy/privileged to be bothered with, where is the support or the "resourcing" that women media makers are supposed to be doing? Not that we're holding our breath or anything. When I ignore you, fail to link to you, not attend your conference, think about why. I'm probably busy living, working, breathing, mami'ing.

Support Can Be Conditional When You're Trans or Queer: An Interview with Katie Kaput and Jennifer Fichter

Victoria Law

Katie Kaput is an anarchist queer transsexual homeschooling mother of two. Jennifer Fichter is a queer mother of three. While in Portland, Oregon, I sat down with them to eat Katie's home-baked vegan chocolate chip cookies and talk about their experiences of motherhood, political work, and movement support (or lack thereof).[1]

Do you—as a mother in the movement—feel supported?

Katie: In general, since I've had my kids, or even since I've started planning to have kids, I feel like support has been very conditional and limited. That probably has a lot to do with the fact that the particular section of the radical community that I've been involved with is queer-focused. It's not just queer, not just radical, but people who are both. When I first had my kids, there was a lot of negativity about the idea of having kids and presumptions that I was going to change my values a lot. People don't want to associate with you or they don't know what to talk to you about. Of course, now a lot of those people have kids.

Jennifer: I feel like childcare is an afterthought or it doesn't happen. When I bring it up, people often say that they hadn't considered it at all. Then, when I press them to have it, they either say they can't because it's too late to come up with something or they come up with some ridiculous thing that's not workable for me or my kids. When I do get support, it's mostly from other moms. We're all trying to make it work together and take care of each other and do things together and hang out together.

---

1. This interview is part of Victoria Law's larger survey of anarchist mamas on parenting and movement support.

What was the extent of your involvement in anarchist projects/organizations before becoming a mother?

Katie: Before I moved away from where I grew up and started trying to have a kid, I was really involved with organizing for Camp Trans. It's a protest/event that happens at the Michigan Women's Music Festival about the exclusion of trans women. Most of the people involved in it are radical beyond just identity politics. There were people from Queer to the Left, which was Chicago anarchists and maybe there were some socialists, and Chicago Lesbian Avengers with which I was involved to some extent. With Chicago Lesbian Avengers, we would participate in other, bigger actions, like events about Mumia or May Day.[2] All my participation was always specifically as a radical person who was queer. For about four years before I had a kid, I was pretty actively involved in planning stuff, like organizing events and raising funds for different actions we were gonna do.

Jennifer: I hung out in the punk scene and got involved in doing some local activism, mostly around gentrification and vegan stuff and Food Not Bombs and anti-patriarchy issues. Most of the activism and radicalism that I've been involved in started more during my first pregnancy.

How did this change during pregnancy or after birth?

Katie: Which I didn't do, but my co-parent did . . . At the same time I decided to have a kid, I moved away from the place where I grew up (Chicago), where I had lots of connections and was really involved, to Portland. In Portland, I found that I couldn't find people who were similar to the people I had been involved with before, like really trans woman positive, radical queer people. While we were here, I felt really isolated because not only was I trans in a not very trans-friendly com-

---

2. World-renowned political prisoner Mumia Abu-Jamal is a radical journalist and former Black Panther convicted of murdering a white Philadelphia police officer in a racially charged 1982 trial deemed unfair by Amnesty International and many others organizations While Mumia's weekly radio essays spotlight injustice everywhere and condemn all forms of oppression, the global "Free Mumia" movement has become a lightning rod for many activist issues including death penalty and prison abolition, anti-war, anti-capitalism, environmental justice, and more. You can find out more at http://www.freemumia.com, http://www.prisonradio.org, and http://www.abu-jamal-news.com.

munity and seeking people who I never found, but also I was in the process of having this kid. That was also something that people that I did meet couldn't really relate to. I didn't know any people who were parents or who were planning to be a parent in Portland. After that, we moved around a lot.

Jennifer: When I lived in Eugene, Oregon, I was speaking up about it and trying to get people to understand and do stuff about it, but . . . there's always some "more important" issue [than] being a parent. It's just always on the back burner . . . It's the last thing that people are interested in because there are so many more interesting things that are happening, especially when people get so involved in things that are happening not even in their own communities, like, "I'm going to go help the Zapatistas in Mexico! But I'm not going to do anything to help the people or the families down the street and create some kind of solidarity right here."

What support have you gotten from the people around you?

Katie: I don't feel that I've experienced a lot of that. Some people went bowling with me and my kids and paid for it. I've repeatedly asked people for childcare so that I can go to events. There's a couple of things I've wanted to go to, one of which happens every month: a Trans Female Spectrum group that has a political focus. They talk about intersectionalities and lots of things that sound really interesting to me, especially in an all trans women/trans female spectrum setting. I would love to have those conversations and I've never had anybody follow through on childcare. People said they would do it and then don't. I've missed it five times now. It's at a time that's not that convenient for me either; it conflicts with my kids' bedtime. I talked to the organizer; she said that maybe they would have a potluck on the weekend sometimes, but that's not a space that's open to my kids because it's exclusively trans female spectrum and neither of my kids qualify, so I *need* childcare to go to it.

Even just to get a break for thinking or going out to do something that's not political, like not even like "Oh, we're at an event and [if] you watch my kid [that] means you'll miss something." Even at things where nobody's missing anything, that hasn't happened.

Jennifer: When I had just had a baby, nobody ever brought food and put it in my fridge, not even other moms. My family lives really far away, so there was no family support either. It was us on our own trying to make everything work—the rent, the bills, etc. I've definitely had people around who were completely clueless, no idea that they should offer to help or how hard it was. I've had hostility, when I've asked, from other activists who were childless. I remember one time this guy came over and he was a pretty big activist in the town. He came over and asked, "What can I do to help you?" I asked him to sweep my kitchen floor because that's easier to do two-handed. He did it but was really mad and later said, "Who do you think you are that you can ask people to come and clean your house for you? I have a house to clean too." So even just getting any kind of basic help, it always seems like I'm a burden and shouldn't ask and whatever help I do get, I should take and be thankful for.

How does gender and sexual identities affect how much support (or lack of support) you've gotten?

Jennifer: I think that people question your parenting abilities more. All kinds of people question you more.

Katie: I can't really tease it all the way out. It's hard to know if people's assumptions about my parenting ability or offers of support or not have anything to do with the fact that I'm trans, which I suspect, or if it's because at first I was nineteen and a high school dropout and broke, or probably some combination. I think the older I get, the less the other stuff comes up because people don't necessarily know that I'm a high school dropout or that I was a parent at nineteen because I don't look as young as I used to. But I definitely have felt that when you're trans or queer (like when you're young or poor or any of the ways that you vary from people's image of what a parent should be), people question your parenting a lot more and feel really entitled to do so. Their support can be conditional based on whether you're living up to what they think you should do in a way that it isn't for people who are, in a lot of cases, almost universally supported.

As a trans woman in queer and feminist radical circles, I often feel this assumption that I am not somehow doing my share or doing things right or that I have all these privileges that other moms don't have or that it couldn't possibly be the case, even though it is, that I am the stay-at-home parent and have all these experiences in common with other moms who aren't trans. There's such an intense narrative in that community of a trans woman as basically being a man who decides, someday in the distant future, to become a woman, which is not at all my experience of myself. I came out way before I had kids and I had kids young and I stayed home with them . . . I feel like, with being trans, there's skepticism whether I've done enough or whether I have an authentic mother experience. I think in general, there's a lot of suspicion around trans women. I don't think it plays out a lot in parenting because most trans women are not young parents, or parents at all necessarily, but I think about it in relation to my life.

And so much of the queer folks, even radical queer folks, so much of what happens is really about the having fun aspect and then there's the political aspect of it, like there may be working together at certain times, but then everyone's going to go to this dance party at this house. I mean, maybe it's the same in straight circles?

I know we talked about this before I fished out the recorder, but can you redescribe some of the childcare and kids' activities at conferences like the ARA childcare and the Gender Spectrum?

Katie: There haven't been any events or conferences that I've been to that have had any childcare at all. So I have no experience with that.

Jennifer: The best childcare that I've seen was in 1997. It was at the National Anti-Racist Action conference in Ohio. They had actual workshops for kids like un-arresting and martial arts. They had dress-up clothes. They paraded through the entire conference making noise and stuff like that. Pregnant moms and kids got to eat first. (There were a *lot* of people at that event, but we got to go to the front of the line and get our food first, which I think is really awesome. That also happens at Rainbow Gatherings.) There was a big march. There were cars along the way with car seats so if any parents or any moms with kids wanted to leave or if things got crazy, there were cars with car seats so they could be taken to a safe location. Parents and kids were protected within the march and kept a certain distance from the Black Bloc but also not put in front of the march where all the media attention would be. And people were making sure to know what was going on all throughout the march so they could know and inform parents and stuff like that. So parents could be *in* the march and kids could be *in* the march and I think that's totally important for kids to experience that and for parents to experience that. I think it is important to think about kids' liberation. It's not just that the moms are being restricted from all these great things, but kids are too. Our kids aren't being able to learn about these things.

At the Gender Spectrum Family conference, there were teen panels of transgendered teens where they talked about their experiences. They had teen workshops the entire time and some [workshops] for even younger kids. They had a large room with a whole rack of dress-up clothes and snacks and games and all kinds of activities for kids the entire time. There was a pool party. There were all sorts of things that were centered around and for kids.

Most of the time we get shoved into a room for two days for sixteen hours; eight hours a day, they're just in a small room with just some coloring books and crayons. I think that those are the two times that stand out in my mind for kid inclusion. That's a whole 'nother radical idea for people—kid inclusion. I've asked for kid inclusion before, not childcare, but have said, "I wanna bring my kid to the workshop. How about that?" and people have said, "Well, they're going to make too much noise. They're going to be distracting and we really don't want kids to be here."

Katie: Which is a parental decision, actually, not a decision for the person doing the workshop.

Jennifer: Yeah, I love it when people make the decision for me and my kids based on what's good for us or not good for us.

Katie: Rio (age seven) was totally paying attention tonight [at a presentation Vikki did about incarceration and resistance in women's prisons]. He said that he learned a bunch. He was definitely interested, but a lot of people would assume that it's not appropriate for him to hear about any of it. It's really good for our kids to learn about what we're doing and what we care about. Whenever he's been involved, in a protest or even in a conversation with people who are informed about stuff, he always feels great.

Jennifer: And kids who are welcome and embraced by radical communities and supported are, I've seen it, from time to time . . . Those kids are always amazing.

Is there anything else you would want to add?

Jennifer: People should ask more how they can support families. It's a common thing in activism [for] radical activists to be like, "I'm going to tell you how I'm going to help you." And it's a longtime [habit] in racial stuff too, like, "I'm going to help those black people." But they don't ask anybody how they want to be helped. They just want to be saviors.

It would be nice for people to say, "How can we support you? How can we help you?" And it's okay for people to say, "I don't know, I want you to figure it out," but it's nice to be asked. That doesn't mean that the parents should organize it all; it means see if parents have anything to say in what they want or need. Also talk to the kids and treat kids like they're actually equal people, and realize that when doing childcare, when supporting kids and parents, kids know a lot what they want too and so you can say to kids, "What do you want to do at this event? What would you value?" They can tell you.

People shuffle kids around a lot and make a lot of decisions for kids and don't do enough inclusion and don't consider them as liberated beings who have choices and desires. I would like to see that happen more. That is really radical and would change our communities. That would change people.

Katie: And kids. It's important to realize that kids can also have seriousness and responsibilities and that a lot of them like it.

Jennifer: It's tough because when there's childcare at an event, but you don't know who those [childcare] people are, you don't want to leave our kids alone with them. Just because someone's at a radical gathering doesn't mean that they can't be a child molester or messed up in the way they treat or talk to your kids. I've definitely had my kids give me feedback all the time and they're like, "That person was a jerk," or, "That person yelled at us or was mean to us." When childcare is offered, it's often just whoever will do it and it's not people who we know or who we know are safe. There has to be some kind of way parents can be assured that these people are safe and accountable.

We have to feel safe that our kids are okay there and the kids have to feel safe.

Performing Allyship:
Notes from a Queer Migrant Parent
a de la maza pérez tamayo

I consider myself privileged to have had an obliging uterus when i decided that i was ready to become a parent. Although adoption had been my first choice, a cursory inquiry rendered that option inaccessible for a number of reasons (among them my migratory status and relative poverty). And so, in the wake of SB1070, i left the abusive relationship i was in and began to turkey baste my way into single parenthood; i was pregnant three months later. I write this with a beautiful three-month-old asleep on my lap and an unsightly stress-induced rash painfully decorating my ribcage.

As a queer, trans, (temporarily) female-bodied, sensory-disabled, neurodivergent, single parent of color with a *migrante* consciousness (and just as many unearned privileges), surrounding myself with politically progressive and socially conscious people has been more of a survival strategy than a personal preference. I compile these not-so-gentle reminders for my friends, elders and lovers who, in their misguided journey to *become* allies rather than *perform* allyship, abandon those of us they seek to stand in solidarity with.

Xenophobia Is Xenophobia, Hipster or Otherwise
The first three White folks whom i told i was pregnant responded with an ostensibly sardonic "oh, anchor-baby?" Contrary to what you may be inclined to think, i don't friend-shop at tea party rallies or KKK socials. In fact, all three were left-of-liberal organizers against the most recent wave of anti-migrant sentiment in Arizona.

Carmen Van Kerckhove, one of the authors at the blog *Racialicious*, defines hipster racism as "ideas, speech, and action meant to denigrate [another person's] race or ethnicity under the guise of being urbane, witty (meaning 'ironic' nowadays), educated, liberal, and/or trendy." The success of my friends' attempt at ironic humor, both dependent on and meant to reinforce my unwavering belief in their position as pro-migrant allies, failed miserably on both counts.

Paternalism Is Genocide's Enabler

When i told my former partner—a White anti-racist organizer working for migrant justice in Arizona—that i had decided to become a parent, she immediately accused me of being selfish. "How can you possibly consider giving birth to a brown baby right now?" she asked. I remember thinking, "what color baby *am* i supposed to have?"

I tried to file my skin off with a nail file when i was five years old. I tried to shave it off a year or two after that. I endured painful monthly regimes of skin bleaching well into my mid-twenties. Somewhere along the way, in the silent interstices between the "wetbacks" and the "beaners," i fell in love with the struggle embedded in my skin. In a world built for White folks—a world that, à la Audre Lorde, we were never meant to survive—communities of color thrive against all odds. Those are the spaces i'm committed to building and maintaining so that one day not too long from now, little a can learn to read (and continue to write) the complex history of his people inscribed on his skin.

Don't Say "Your Body, Your Choice" When You Really Mean "Your Body, Your Choice . . . Unless It's Not the Same as My Choice, in Which Case Fuck You, Your Body, and Your Choice"

I lost several budding friendships to my birthing choice. After months of careful consideration (and more gender dysphoria than i had originally anticipated), i decided that the best thing for my bodily and psychological well-being was to have a C-section. I suppose it's entirely possible that i missed the memo entitled "You're a Raging Misogynist Unless You Deliver Vaginally," but several White feminists who had provided helpful resources about homebirths and midwifery were quick to inform me that my choice made me an illiterate enemy to uterus-bearers everywhere. Apparently, i had committed a double faux-pas: the first in choosing to give birth in a hospital, and the second in not wanting to push a fetus out into legal personhood.

Let's get a few things cleared up: as a migrant of color, the complexity of my relationship to the state apparatus likely differs from that of most White citizens. For instance, while the hospital registered my baby for me, delivering at home would've entailed going to the Department of Health Services in anti-migrant Arizona. Visits to state institutions carry an increased threat of deportation that, however small, i am unwilling to risk as a single parent. As a trans person, my relationship to my reproductive capabilities likely differs from that of most normative cisgender women. Not everyone with a vagina has a birth canal.

As a queer person who prefers the latter end of S&M, my relationship to pain likely differs from most hetero- or homonormatively sexual people's. My scars tell stories, and this one is a gentle reminder of the day we fell in love.

For folks aspiring to perform allyship, be humble enough to:

- keep oppressive opinions to yourself (but, by all means, work them out later in the mirror or among similarly privileged folks)
- understand that if you don't get it, it may not be for you to get
- above all, take a moment to celebrate the revolutionary love involved in parenting for collective liberation.

On Fear and Commitments
Mustafa Shukur

From age fifteen to around thirty, I was intent on never having children. As a young man, I felt vulnerable and afraid of commitment; I had not found a consistent partner or cared to look for one and perceived that security is achieved by isolation.

My main purpose in life was to escape the construct of culture shock, familial remediation, and class identity. My comfort depended on the incarceration of my emotions: love no one, not even yourself.

I traveled a lot when I was young. My father was a PhD candidate of Journalism at the University of Exeter in the 1980s, and we spent a lot of time in England. I grew up there and identified with "western" concepts of tragedy, comedy, family, security, and luxury.

Long before England, we had run through most of Europe and every Arabic speaking country (West Asia, North Africa). My father settled in England when the Iraqi government paid his way and gave him the chance to achieve a PhD to further his career. He was already Chief of Staff at a major Iraqi news agency.

In Exeter, I found myself. I became self-aware; life was fair on occasion, though there was more external influence than internal scruples. I was called "nigger," based on my brownish tint. Other than being very offensive, I was not aware of the meaning of the word, nor, I assume, were the kids who said it.

I got into a few fights, but nothing too dramatic. I had crushes and I was crushed on. The teachers, the headmaster loved me. I was English; I had no idea who I was.

In 1987, Father PhD moved us back to Iraq. I was in a panic, and I cried that I would miss my friends. To me, Iraq was a desolate desert: I was sure it would be hot, humid, and the people stupid, an uneducated mix of thugs.

I was unaware of the clash of civilizations, but it had imbued itself early into my psyche and I, like most of the working class prejudices, became a statistic. We spent two years in Baghdad at the height and nigh deconstruction of the Iran/Iraq war, living under beds, invasion sirens blaring, surface to air missile dunes a few hundred yards from our house. I missed Exeter, where it was normal. During those two years, my parents went through a serious hell of bitter hatred, anger, and resentment, eventually leading up to a divorce. My older (by two years) brother and I went back and forth between extended families since our parents could not stand to be in the same house together. In 1989, the Iraqi news agency sent my father to New York City, and my parents decided to reconcile, saving face for their young children. I was twelve. My mother became pregnant again and my younger brother, Ali, was born in August of that year in the States.

I had my first real experience with children. Ali was small at the hospital, quiet yet resolute. My mother looked wasted and spent, but I never took into account what she went through three times in her life. Now that I think about it, she probably received better medical care in Baghdad in 1976 and 1974 than she did in New York City in 1989.

I changed diapers, warmed bottles, and nurtured and played with the child. As he grew older, I was his prototype and I just wanted to ignore him. Our family spent birthdays together, but we did not really observe holidays. I can still remember my parents being bitter with each other. I can imagine they did not wish to observe holidays together with children they did not really want.

In my adolescence, I became detached from myself, from my obligations, responsibility; I found alcohol and cigarettes to be suitable habits. But what sort of obligations would a twelve-year-old have at that point?

When Ali was eight, then twelve, and I was in my twenties, he came to exhibit the same tendencies I had held at this age. I was his role-model. I felt Ali could have had a different life had I not been involved or had I been involved differently in his rearing. I was withdrawn from him when he needed a male connection to the world. Understandably, father was lacking in expertise where a PhD could not oblige: this experience has to be lived and breathed, not taught. I made a terrible mistake. Forcing my little brother to become independent during his own adolescence was counterproductive and it has estranged us. What he needed was a support structure, bouncing ideas and liquid thought, malleable and non-hierarchical observation. I failed him.

I was drawn into activism when I was around twenty-five. I thought having children would impede the action of "permanent revolution," and I felt already too old to raise children. I also felt a concern for their safety: how could I bring a child to life, forcing them to become statistics and victims?

Fast-forward to age thirty-three: I have been partnered for four months with a woman who is the very definition of political experience and fortitude. An Anarchist meets a reformed Socialist (i.e., borderline Anarchist). Her experiences with family are much different than mine, but those are her stories to tell. She became pregnant at age thirty-four, in a relationship with a man who never wanted children, never wanted to commit to her, and was afraid of being in a corner with no exits. Her strength in me and our existence made it an easy choice for me to believe in our decision.

My assurances to my child and my family now are much different than I expected them to be. My regrets: that our relationship together was not long before she got pregnant; that our child will never see Baghdad the way I saw it; that I never gave Iraq the chance it deserved to be remembered. My paternal grandfather, I have come to learn, was Governor of Fallujah back when Britain imposed itself on Iraq. He prepared speeches and organized the community to resist the occupation and kicked the British out. Fallujah under the current "western" occupation was the first to resist and hit back the hardest. In Fallujah, the charred bodies of Blackwater street-level capitalists were hung from bridges.

I have no regrets concerning my son, my family, and our future together. I expect there to be extreme difficulties, major highs and lows, though I can safely say that I cannot perceive an exit strategy.

We have both learned from our childhoods what to change in our current lifestyles and we aim to not regurgitate a self-perpetuating cycle.

Laith is a happy baby.

My fears are ever changing. When I held them both and helped them into our home from the hospital, I was afraid I would drop him. He was so tiny. That fear surrendered to confidence. I'm afraid I would make the same mistakes I had done with Ali. I'm afraid I may yell at Laith and he will never forgive me. I am trying to change my atypical patriarchal heritage to create an existence of less individualistic selfishness for my son, my Anarcho-Pagan wife/partner, and myself. I don't want to be withdrawn, dissociated. Most of all, I will not stand to be apolitical.

My biggest fear is how to raise a child in the States. It will be an ardent task in a context of aggression against Islam/Arabs, xenophobia, "terror babies" watch, heavy racism, fear of cultural appropriation and preservation of native culture, and hearing how his classmate's father/mother/brother/sister/aunt/uncle died at the hands of the insurgency which he calls the Resistance. I think of the community where we will plant ourselves in the coming years, a community full of multicultural, multilingual people that will provide a feeling of security and support. If we were to remain in Austin for the duration of Laith's education, the support structure to which he will belong will look like a salad rather than a melting pot. All individuals are unique, not cast to a liquid formation, self-perpetuating normal salient theory and delegitimizing "ethnic" identities. What does normal look like, anyway?

I believe it is important to be immersed in discussions on heritage, culture, "rights and responsibilities" of all people. Here in Texas, the Board of Education has identified potential exclusions from our history books, trying to rewrite the "impact of the Progressive Era."[1] This is what Laith will be learning; his classmates will have no history lessons on progressive Arabs and the influence of Islam and Persia on European Enlightenment. Later, he may feel even more marginalized from his peers when he realizes that his parents are bisexual and communist-anarchists.

Even as I contemplate the multiple types of marginalization that our kids will encounter and have to struggle against as they grow, I realize that despite my fears about parenting, I have no regrets about having a child.

---

1. For more info: http://news.firedoglake.com/2010/05/18/radical-re-imagining-of-history-by-the-texas-school-board-of-education/.

Four
COLLECTIVE
ACTION

When child care organizing is not integrated with the organizing of the rest of the event, the work of the child care committee remains invisible to those who plan the rest of the event. Since the child care is arranged and carried out by child care specialists, collective members who have not previously been held responsible for children learn nothing about the work child care involves . . .

Throughout our society the work involved in child care is underestimated and undervalued. Children and their caretakers are hidden in homes, schools, and day care centers. Professional child care workers are underpaid, and mothers are not paid at all . . .

When we isolate and ignore those who accept responsibility for the child care at our events, when we give them too much to do and too little respect for what they do, what is the result? Burned out child care workers and dismal child care. —Mary Wallace, Lee MacKay, and Dorrie Nagler, *Children and Feminism* (Vancouver: Lesbian and Feminist Mothers Political Action Group, 1987).

How have different collectives addressed issues of children and family? Banding together, individual parents have organized and demanded space to ensure their children's safety and inclusion in larger protests. Radical collectives publicly recognize the importance of mothering while also sharing knowledge about reproductive justice with other mothers. Realizing that support is not only crucial to involvement in social justice organizing, but can also be the deciding factor in participation, activists have formed radical childcare collectives to meet the needs of the families in their midst. Childcare collectives have started in cities such as Atlanta, Baltimore, New York City, and Washington, DC.

Across the city, many women of color led projects recognize kids and families as integral to movement building. Inspired by these projects, a group of organizers pulled together Regeneración. We participate in child-raising as a form of resistance that builds radical communities and relationships. —Regeneración, "What Is Regeneración?" 2007 (http://www.childcarenyc.org/?q=node/2)

A Message from Mamas of Color Rising and Young Women United: Mother's Day, May 2010

We believe women have the right to choose if, when, and how they become mothers.

On this Mother's Day, we want more than flowers and cards. We want all mothers (including poor mothers, undocumented mothers, young mothers, queer mothers and single mothers) to have the power and the access to choose their birthing option. We believe that all women have the right to choose a birth option that is healthiest for themselves and their families. We also believe that all women have a right to accurate information about birthing options and equal access to hospital, birth center, and home birth services.

In the United States, maternal and infant mortality rates are alarmingly high, particularly within communities of color. Research shows that holistic prenatal care (including nutrition and health education) from early pregnancy on, as well as continuous labor support during birth, contributes to healthier outcomes for both mothers and babies. These options, inherent to the midwifery model of care, are not available to poor women (uninsured or on Medicaid) in Texas or many other states throughout the country. While Medicaid will cover midwife-attended births in New Mexico, information and access to the full range of birthing options is greatly shaped by a woman's race and class. On Mother's Day 2010, Mamas of Color Rising (MOCR) and Young Women United (YWU) collaborated on a joint day of action and awareness.

Most poor and working class mothers of color don't have access to information on all of our potential birthing options. For Mother's Day, we took our Birth Justice message to the streets in our local communities to honor mamas of color with flowers as a form of creative outreach on birthing rights and birthing options.

MOCR wanted to raise awareness in their Austin communities about the midwifery model care, currently inaccessible for most women of color in Texas. MOCR decided they would hand out flowers to women of color with a card attached listing [the top ten] reasons that

Medicaid in Texas *should* cover midwifery care.

The list read:

10. Helps to prevent unnecessary interventions (technology, drugs, and surgery)
9. Provides continuous support (midwives stay with you through-out labor and delivery)
8. Healthier babies
7. Promotes bonding with mother and child
6. Promotes breastfeeding
5. Supports mother's and baby's physical and emotional well-being
4. Cheaper prenatal, delivery, and postnatal care
3. Continuous prenatal and postnatal care
2. Safer birth for mother and baby
1. Mother holds the power (she has a more active voice in her pregnancy and birth)

YWU moved to share information about Medicaid coverage of all birth options in New Mexico, where it is a woman's right to choose between a homebirth, birth center birth, or hospital birth.

Mamas' Action in Austin

The Austin Mamas gathered in a parking lot of a grocery store that they thought would be supportive of their work, as the majority of their customers are families and women of color. However, the store managers failed to demonstrate interest in their work. Nonetheless, the Mamas, being the revolutionary group that they are, continued their outreach in the parking lot, aware that their presence was not wanted.

As the members of MOCR approached women of color in the parking lot, they offered each woman a flower to acknowledge the work that they do/did as a mother. Some were surprised, perplexed, responsive; the majority were thankful. Some even offered donations for the flower. It was clarified by a Mama that no donation was needed and that the flower was simply a symbol of acknowledgement and appreciation from one woman of color to another.

MOCR passed out nearly 300 carnations to women before the store security approached and notified them that they were not allowed to pass out flowers in the parking lot.

Mamas' Action in Albuquerque

The Albuquerque Mamas gathered in a community park where many families of color hang out. As expected, the park was full of celebrating families on Mother's Day. The YWU Mamas made their way through the park, stopping to give flowers to mamas and women, along with a handout on birthing options in New Mexico. Women seemed to appreciate the flowers and were interested in the information we were sharing.

Among our YWU mamas in the park were one of New Mexico's few midwives of color, who catches babies at home, and some home-birth mamas who had birthed babies at home. Some women with whom YWU connected that day found the idea of homebirth a new one, but thought it was an interesting option.

After passing out 200 bunches of flowers, YWU Mamas found each other and their children, gave thanks for the day, and made their ways back home.

Reclaim the Commons
Maxina Ventura

When we became aware of the biotech convention in downtown San Francisco planned for June 2004, a bunch of us organizers from Circle A Cluster and Reclaiming (a Pagan group) got together and said, "Time for a response. Let's do it!" We planned for a weeklong convergence, and rented a warehouse a couple blocks from the convention center for two weeks.

A couple of us parents realized that we needed to be in on the organizing of anything in which we wanted to participate or else things were not likely to end up particularly family-accessible.

We put out a call for other parents to be part of organizing these actions and to call ourselves Radical Family Collective. We started by making it a priority that we had a specific kid zone space as part of the convergence center. It was not generally set up as a drop-off/babysitting scene, but rather a place to have as a cool-out area, a place where kids could nap, parents could meet and watch each other's kids for each other, and families could do art.

When we got together to divvy up spaces within the warehouse, people without kids predictably assumed that the kids should be in a room way back in the bowels of the place (out of sight, out of mind, it seemed). We were assertive, pushy even, in refusing that spot and insisted that, for various reasons, we needed the little room right up front. I pointed out that, for one, kids would be in the most danger in case of a cop riot in the convergence center if we were stuck all alone back there. Up front, everyone would be aware if anything were about to happen and we could quickly get the kids out. RFC had also strategized that it was important to have it out to the media that there was a kid zone at the convention center. Not only would that welcome families, but it would alert the cops that the convergence center would have families in residence. All in all, we realized that we could help safeguard everyone and our convergence center by our very existence in the space. So we had the room up front and a huge banner outside the place announcing the kid zone. No cop attacks happened at the center.

During the week of actions, the convergence center was a site for good food, play, meetings, art, massages, first aid, and media access. There was a 1,000-square foot permaculture garden in a room with a wall of windows. It was gorgeous, and truly beautiful and calming, with fountains and barrels of remediation mix to be stirred by anyone along the way to oxygenate it. Obviously, community can be built more easily when people both work and play together, so we had all that good stuff happening under one roof and in close proximity to some of the street actions.

Another thing we wanted to do for/with parents was to create ways to make us feel safer about going out as families to street actions, fully assuming our right to do so, but also knowing we'd be facing a load of pissed-off and violent cops. So we offered a one-day legal workshop for families with the lure that we had a movement lawyer willing to offer services to any parent arrested *if* she/he had attended this workshop. At the workshop, parents got to learn more about possible results if they intentionally risked arrest or if they were swept up and arrested without intending to be arrested, and about how to be reunited with kids as quickly as possible. Parents filled out consent forms allowing kids to be released to the people who were listed on the sheet and provided emergency contact info. We kept that info with us in case of any sweeps, so we could work with the lawyer to make calls and track people if any planned or unplanned arrests occurred.

While only a small group attended that meeting, it was worthwhile for everyone involved and great to be able to include it in advertising as another way to have families be present in people's minds as part of the action, not just tagging along.

During that week, the feedback to our simple kid zone was generally fabulous, as non-parents were really happy to have kids around and liked the family vibe. There were a few crotchety people who, once the action was over, didn't want kids at meetings, however. There was a big scene about this at our post-action evaluation meeting. People would say things like, "We really want kids here, but they should be in another room." Then there were the comments about how kids can be disruptive, which outraged and amused us parents. We pointed out that we'd rarely been to a meeting where some adult hadn't interrupted a meeting or somehow made it go on longer than planned. And if we're talking revolution, do we expect a revolution to occur if we send away the next generation to pick their toenails in some church basement with some adult (probably one of the parents) who then also misses the meeting? It was rotten and, as a result, not too many parents came to subsequent actions.

We have to push hard on this, as parents are getting isolated. A whole middle generation's decades of experience get lost and younger people keep reinventing the wheel, even though often they would be perfectly happy to stop reinventing a wheel to do something more useful and add something newer to the mix. For those of us who are single parents with no other parent at home even as an option to stay home with the kids (not what we were seeing as optimal, to be sure), the message I often get is, "Oh, well, bummer. Well, you decided to have kids."

Revolution sure won't be handed to us, or made for us . . . we have to shape it as we will.

Experiencing Critical Resistance 10 (CR10) Through the Children's Program

Kate Shapiro

My relationship with the 2009 CR10: Strategy and Struggle to Abolish the Prison Industrial Conference began the year before when I was invited to work with the folks from Regeneración Childcare in New York to build an abolitionist children's program.[1] Having met and worked with some of the Regen folks through the Children's Social Forum process at the 2007 US Social Forum (USSF), we immediately began splashing around with expansive and textured plans for the Children's Program. We agreed from the beginning that we wanted it to be magic—to create a space where we were all engaging together through story, song, imagination while also recognizing and holding all of the different places and experiences we were. It is not that we wanted to suspend reality, but rather create realities within our realities with the goal that everyone participating in the Children's Program would understand or relate to the prison-industrial complex in different ways that were grounded in legacy, resistance, creativity, and hope.[2]

I was thrilled to participate: to begin to push further these conversations around movement building and abolition through play and political education with young people, to push forward the thinking and

1. The Regeneración Childcare Collective is committed to growing an intergenerational movement for collective liberation. Regeneración Childcare NYC participates in childraising as a form of resistance that builds radical communities and relationships by providing childcare at organizational meetings and events and in collaboration with other childcare collectives. For more info, see: http://www.childcarenyc.org. "Abolition" refers to the movement to abolish prisons and the prison system.

2. The term "prison-industrial complex" (PIC) refers to the ways that the United States uses prisons and policing as a failed "solution" to social, political, and economic problems. The PIC depends upon the oppressive systems of racism, classism, sexism, and homophobia. It includes human rights violations, the death penalty, industry and labor issues, policing, courts, media, community powerlessness, the imprisonment of political prisoners, and the elimination of dissent. The PIC is also fueled by dramatic and racist reporting about "crime," "delinquency," and "rebellion," creating a culture of fear and the belief that increased imprisonment is necessary for public and personal safety.

knowledge we developed when building the Children's Social Forum at the USSF . . . but to have a year instead of three months, to have fifteen brilliant minds and bodies instead of one or two, to have a budget! What! I was also politically intrigued to learn more about the work of Critical Resistance and hoped to strengthen and string together what often feel like disparate pieces of my life and work and politics—organizing, youth work, and childcare!

What we ended up creating was a play.[3] The play was the frame for the program and in this play we all went on a magical adventure with each other where we met a number of different young people:

Akila: A Black American whose grandmother was a Black Panther. Akila's power is that of knowledge, knowing the histories of oppression and resistance.

Luna: A Navajo girl living on the Reservation whose mom was taken by the Prison Monster because they thought she was crazy. Luna's power is that she can create anything from the earth.

Jadu: A mixed Black, Chinese and Indian from Trinidad, living in Mississippi. Jadu's power is that he is a dreamer who has powerful visions.

Esperanza: A Latina transwoman who hangs on The Pier of NYC with a community of other queer and genderqueer folks of color. Esperanza's power, along with her community, is that they are shape-shifters.

Eli: A white genderqueer Jewish person. Eli is an ally whose special power is empathy and feeling; Eli knows that it is important to bring people together.

Each of the characters has a specific power as well as a specific relationship with the Prison Monster, who represents the prison-industrial complex. Akila gets put into juvenile detention after a night of nightmares haunted by the prison monster.

While in juvie, she sees that the prison monster is collecting everyone's dreams and locking them into a huge vault. The dream of a magic carpet escapes the vault. Akila quickly scoops it up and *escapes*. She then

---

3. For more about the play, see http://www.childcarenyc.org/?q=node/12.

meets to rest of the characters and they share stories: Jadu's family was deported in ICE raids, Luna's mother was taken away for being "crazy," and Luna was put into foster care, Esperanza and her friends are policed and criminalized for being trans and gender non-conforming. After we met each new character in the play, we stopped and did an activity—some were full-group and some were more age-specific—and then came back together for the next scene of the play.

With the CR10 children's program, different ideas were woven throughout the play as well as all the activities, and it had an amazing tone! Everyone loved the prison monster play and the dots were connected. The second part of the program was devoted to strengthening our powers: healing the land and each other and eventually we all dismantled the prison monster together!

During CR10, I was pretty sick, feverish, and also overwhelmed at all of my loves in the same place at the same time. I wasn't present for the whole program because I was helping to hold down some of the logistical pieces and also because I was sick and not wanting to infect any little ones. There were folks from Regeneración childcare and the San Francisco Childcare Collective as well as a young lovely person from a newly started DC Childcare Collective, so it was a great informal meeting of the minds. There was a powerful fluidity in the group over the weekend as we all worked to balance out our individual needs and responsibilities to ourselves, our wellness and other folks/events at the conference . . . it was almost as though the program took on a life of its own, with individuals able to flow in and out without stress or guilt as they needed to.

As we have moved forward, some questions have arisen: What does it mean to come together for short amounts of time, often as strangers (like the participants of the children's program), in an overwhelming and overstimulating environment and then return to our homes? How do we build continuity and momentum as we continue to collaborate on these magical politicized, often transient, young people centered spaces? This is at the core of the work!

While I did not attend very many adult workshops, it was powerful to primarily understand or interact with the conference through the Children's Program. In some ways, I think I might prefer it. It helped me stay more grounded. It's not that I don't love grown folks (I do!), but, in my experience, conferences are often very fractured and buzzy with everyone shuttling around to different two-hour sessions. Many SONG folks speak about how thinking and engaging in skill transfer for only one or two hours together doesn't always provide an opportunity to go deep in addressing challenges or political strategies, skills or thinking.[4] I often leave not feeling filled up or satiated. What often *does* fill me up is the conversations way too late into the night with new friends, informal mentors, and other random brilliant folks.

The powerful fluidity of the Children's Program at CR10, the way the program and organizers were able to expand and contract, wasn't co-incidental. It was definitely built out of shared work over time by groups and pairs of people who have been working together in our homeplaces or in different movement spaces, as well as out of the immense amount of labor over the year that went into crafting the days. It was magical for all of us. We weren't creating a space only *for* young people but a space where all of us—young people, parents, non-youth, volunteers, guardians—were given the space to transform together. Even for a short amount of time, *this* is the true power of conference spaces: to live and breathe magic, to dream and act and transform together so that we can all go home to the work and struggle a little more filled up and with the knowledge in our bodies that dream and play and magic and creativity are necessary for our strategies and practices in building the world we know we need.

---

4. SONG, or Southerners on New Ground, is a Southern regional organization made up of working-class, people of color, immigrants, and rural LGBTQ people. See http://southernersonnewground.org/ for more information.

Whose City? KIDZ CITY!

Sine Hwang Jensen, Harriet Moon Smith, and China Martens

Sine: Early Saturday morning, St John's Church, also known as the 2640 Space, was beginning to hum with the sounds of the 2009 City From Below conference in Baltimore. People bustled behind book tables, served up food and coffee, began contemplating neo-liberalism and resistance; everywhere was hustle and buzz. I didn't know what the day would bring, and I didn't know that Kidz City was actually going to be the best imaginable way to start it.

That morning, two kids were occupying Kidz City—Siu Loong and Pop. Siu Loong's mom was participating in a panel about prisons and policing. Pop's dad is a member of the United Workers, a worker-led workers' economic justice and human rights movement in Baltimore.

I spent the first few hours of Kidz City amongst the Zapatista *bordados*, sharing coloring books, snacks and art supplies, and playing a pink guitar with a missing string with Siu Loong. Later, I drew a picture of a flying cat creature whom Pop named "Butt Butt Booty Butt." Clearly, the first song we played for the radical sing-along then was Kimya Dawson's "Alphabutt" and we had so much fun singing about farts that we played that song over and over!

Later in the afternoon, I happened upon the Exploding Seed Time Machine story led by Tom Kertes of the United Workers. The room was packed! Donning their one-of-a-kind time machine hats, the kids were making their trip with Harriet Tubman escaping the plantation on the Underground Railroad. I also hung out with Kidz City outside for the Genderful World! workshop with Owen, Abby, and Jacob. In a genderful world, boys can be ballerinos, we can paint pictures of our dreamselves, and we can wear whatever gendered clothing we please!

The importance of Kidz City to building an inclusive radical conference was paramount. To me, exploring the City From Below meant exploring the ways in which marginalized city dwellers can be not only a part, but in charge of shaping their environment, their lives, and their destinies. Sure, having childcare at a conference is about convenience, compassion, and kindness. But politically, it's about allowing the space for caretakers, especially womyn, to be a part of the conference and to actually involve, not just preoccupy, children in the struggle for Radical-evolution. It is power that allows us to choose which voices to hear, and which voices to silence. Children are not only the future, they are the present, too. Their voices need to be heard, no matter how loud, weird-sounding or disruptive they seem to be. It was unbelievably rewarding to work towards creating a space for those voices to boom.

• • •

Harriet: The day before the conference, we cleaned and rearranged the space for childcare. The space was in great need of some cheering up. Wind chimes, cloth hangings, posters, rugs, pillows, throw blankets, and lamps were brought in to brighten and make the space more welcoming. We loaded the room's only table with books, crayons, paper, markers, games, jump ropes, a Frisbee, sewing supplies, paint (both for paper and faces), and other miscellaneous activity supplies. At the opening panel on Friday night, we claimed a part of the main room for Kidz City. The task was to make a banner that would announce our city to visitors for the next two days. There were two people who had just arrived from Toronto; they were about an hour early for the panel discussion, so we chatted and sewed together. Many people's hands worked on our banner and made it the unique artwork that marked the entrance of Kidz City.

There was a special brunch Sunday morning that was supposed to take place at Participation Park. Unfortunately, it was raining too hard to hold it there. The worm bin show-and-tell and seed bomb making were to take place inside at the rain location. There were no takers for these activities. So we held the activities back at the main location a few hours later, after the regular conference was back in session. It was a lot of fun and there was some wonderful enthusiasm about the worms, composting, and seed bombing the neighborhood.

Later, we held a sidewalk exploration fairyland extravaganza that was delightful. The energy from this workshop did not end until all the children went home. In some cases, the children protested leaving and said they couldn't wait to come back. All in all, it was a beautiful weekend!

I want to continue to think about access to spaces by parents and children. We should be thinking: how would our communities benefit or be different if these voices, which are so often missing in our conversations and our events, were heard? It's not a favor that we are providing as people without kids to those who do. It is our privilege and it benefits us, too. Since the coordination of childcare tends to fall on the women of our society, women's voices, mothers' voices, but also fathers' and others', are missing from so many of the events I attend.

More and more, I am noticing this absence, as well as my own ease in moving through my day not having to worry if spaces are unfriendly to children or how people will react to kids in my care. I think that, as we seek a more just society using the principles of anarchism, feminism, racial justice, and others, we cannot leave out the voices of parents, aunties, uncles, grandparents, children, and others. It will be difficult and it will require a lot of learning on my part (and maybe your part too), but it will be worth it.

• • •

China: The children's programming (seven workshops, two of which were for all ages) turned out exceedingly well and was enjoyed by all! We integrated the themes of the bigger conference into our own programs. It was also a chance for all ages to mingle and work together to share care and support everyone's needs. Said one local mother: "I was impressed with how into it the children were and how into the children the volunteers were."

During the rainy Saturday, we mostly stayed inside our basement headquarters. Jenny Sage's "Pockets and Patches" class had children and adults gasping, "Ohhhh!" and "Ahh!" as she showed how tennis shoes could become part of shirts and that pants could turn into skirts. "But no matter how wonderful something is," I said as I dragged out our collection of boxes into the tiny stairwells outside for two restless "bored" youngsters to create their robot/spaceship box city within, "not everyone is going to want to do it."

Owen Smith, another childcare provider, chimed in, "And that's okay, right?"

When the sun came out on Sunday, we were glad to expand into the courtyard where our workshops took place in the glorious spring sunshine.

Kidz City had constant Spanish-to-English translation throughout the weekend for Lupita, a Spanish-speaking girl who traveled from North Carolina with El Kilombo and her family.

We pushed the norms in other ways, too. When a little boy tried to pull a pink ribbon off Owen's head, saying that he shouldn't wear it, Owen said that he liked to wear a pink ribbon and that boys can wear anything they like. This example soon led to the child deciding he would like to wear a pink ribbon on his head, too. In such an environment, many different discussions came up and were explored in ways one doesn't always see in other places.

We had some difficulties, of course. For example, although translation was widely cited as something many adults were impressed with and enjoyed, we had to scramble to find Spanish translators for each shift, sending someone upstairs to ask for a translator or patching together what we could from other bilingual volunteers or the friends around us. We also needed to be more organized in some ways. It would have helped to stress pre-registration, to have had a volunteer orientation, and to print out a set of guidelines for everyone. We've had a lot of discussions on what worked and what we could improve for next time, which continued after the weekend was over.

In fact, organizing together contained so much excitement, inspiration, brainstorming new ideas and putting them into practice in ways that we haven't seen before that we have decided not to stop. We have decided to keep meeting as a radical childcare collective.

As Elliot Liu, my co-presenter from the Children and the City workshop, said, "Doing childcare is a chance to put your politics into practice." At the end of the conference, two people said to me, "Next conference I go to, I am definitely going to volunteer to do childcare!"

Homefulness

Tiny a.k.a. Lisa Gray-Garcia

From Removal to Reparations . . .
From Houselessness to HOMEFULNESS . . .
From indigenous lands stolen to budget crumbs thow-en-
From affordable housing in name only to rights to a roof by any means
necessary . . .
From the cult of independence to the Revolution of inter-dependence . . .
From poverty-pimped housing po-lice to Revolutionary equity for all
Realized . . . !!!!

After 500 years of removal, GentriFUKation, Anthro-Wrong-ology, akkkademik studies and philanthro-pimped capitalist compromises, and consumerist destruction POOR Magazine's family of landless, indigenous elders, ancestors, mamas, aunties, uncles, fathers and *abuelitos,* daughters, and sons will be realizing the revolution that is Homefulness.

The 1st HOMEFULNESS site includes sweat-equity co-housing for four to ten landless, houseless/landless families in poverty, as well as a site for PeopleSkool, a multigenerational, multi-lingual school based on an indigenous model of teaching and learning, POOR Magazine peoples media center, Uncle Al & Mama Dee's Social justice and Arts cafe and *tierra madre* garden where we will hopefully grow food for the whole community.

The process to dream and build HOMEFULNESS will be a community-led one with indigenous scholars, lived scholars, and formally edukkkated scholars respecting and working together to create a re-mix of design, sustainability, and off-grid self-determination.

How did this finally happen?

Revolutionary Change Session launches true Change . . . Crumbling the Myth
of The Gift—Deconstructing Donor Denial & Dismantling The Non-Profit

Industrial Complex
. . . One Outcome at a Time

Launched on Juneteenth of 2009 the POOR Magazine **Revolutionary Change Session** was a moment in herstory, a poor people-led/indigenous people-led teach-in for conscious folk with race, class and/or education privilege who were interested in exploring, implementing and practicing truly revolutionary expressions of giving, equity sharing and change.

At this herstoric event poverty, in/migrante, race, elder, youth, disability and indigenous skolaz presented curriculum on the kkkriminalization of poor peoples and public space, local and global poverty, ableism, welfare, border fascism/false borders, systems abuse, underground economic strategies, po'lice brutality, profiling, globalization, gentriFUKation, indigenous removal and more.

The Revolutionary Change Session birthed POOR Magazine's Solidarity Board

POOR Magazine's Solidarity Board was formed by conscious young folks with different forms of race, class and/or akkkademik privilege whose perspectives were skooled by Poverty Scholarship at the Revolutionary Change Session and other teachings, action and prayer that grew from that space. From this skooling each became interested in POOR Magazine's analysis of reparations and resistance and began to work on decolonizing their resources.

Two years later, POOR Magazine's Solidarity Board gathered enough of the blood-stained Amerikkkan Dollaz to facilitate a "purchase" of stolen land on Turtle Island to begin the healing of our mama (*pachamama*) to begin the healing of our communities suffering from the violence and pain of poverty, racism, budget genocide, paper trail theft and GentriFUKation, to begin the healing of our children and our families, ancestors and elders through equity redistribution, dekkkolonization, prayer and ceremony.

To ask permission, to cleanse, to pray, to meet, to heal . . .

In the ways of our ancestors first we must walk softly on our (Pacha)Mama and in this East Oakland community, where many of POOR Magazine's family members have been gentrified out of, or currently dwell houselessly or in different forms of at-risk housing, we must introduce ourselves to the land and the peoples of this intentionally blighted, scandalously speculated on, po'lice brutalized, and long ago forgotten community in poverty and ask permission in ceremony to build the Revolution that is HOMEFULNESS.

As an act of resistance to the hierarchal and unjust distribution of wealth and resources locally and globally, POOR Magazine is formerly calling the fundraising effort for HOMEFULNESS, an Equity Campaign, instead of a Capital Campaign, as through equity sharing, not tied to financial resources, we will be creating permanent and lasting solutions to houselessness for families in poverty who have been displaced, evicted, gentrified and destabilized out of their indigenous lands and communities.

For more information on how to become involved with this project, please call 415-863-6306 or to go: http://www.poormagazine.org/.

Mothers Among Us: The Prison Birth Project

Marianne Bullock

The Prison Birth Project is an organization focused on reproductive justice. We work to provide education, support, and advocacy to women and girls at the intersection of the criminal justice system and motherhood. Our goal is to provide the tools to help them make empowering choices and to provide continuous care throughout the spectrum of pregnancy, birth, and postpartum. We offer this in the form of childbirth education classes, one on one meeting time, our Mothers Among Us program and open resource compilation with local organizations and knowledgeable references. We seek to provide a transformational space for women to support each other and work through issues of oppression that affect their families and the social landscape of mothering.

Many of us hold values in our hearts that support the abolition of the prison and criminal system and support movements of decarceration and alternatives to jail sentences. This system wasn't built for women and current policies in no way support family creation. Lots of people ask me how I can hold those views and still work within an institution that does not support mothers/families. The answer for me is simple: you don't leave your friends behind.

Over the past two years, we have identified five areas within prison policy that most affect incarcerated women. You can support them through their own prisoner-led movements and by supporting outside movements to change these policies:

1. Lack of access to healthy, nutritious food
2. Lack of visitation with children and family/lack of transportation for children to facility
3. Use of restraints while pregnant during delivery and postpartum
4. Use of medical isolation while postpartum
5. Lack of sound breastfeeding policy and support for new mothers who wish to breastfeed their babies

As I write this, I am on-call for a woman who is exactly forty weeks pregnant. This will be her third baby and may be the only child of whom she retains custody. My job as a doula has been to support her in navigating the decisions that she has to make for the health of herself and her child. The organization I work for advocates for mothers to retain their custodial rights and give birth in the most empowering way possible, even while behind the wall.

For the past two years, most of the births through which I have supported mamas have been for women who will be leaving their babies about forty-eight hours after they deliver. Despite this, in almost all cases, the delivery room has been like any other: filled with love, joy, fear, pain, release, and beauty. It is after the baby is born, during the days when a mother's hormones shift and start to dip, that a mom goes back to jail. I go with her to offer her what little support I can.

Lots of mothers are put in medical isolation after they deliver and are unable to gain support from the friends and community inside that they have made for themselves. I've thought a lot about how to support mothers in their transition back to jail (and away from their new baby) and have sat down, one on one, with many of them to figure out exactly what they need (other than to be with their babies). Here is the list that we came up with:

Ten Ways to Support Incarcerated Mamas Postpartum:
1. Write them letters! Show them the light at the end of the tunnel!
2. Send them pictures of their babies, cards, and pretty pictures.
3. Give them a journal.
4. Lend an ear, talk directly about the loss of the child physically right now, and don't try to relate unless you have *been there*!
5. Go to court dates, show the judge that there are people who care, and people watching the decisions he/she is making.
6. Put money in commissary/phone fund.
7. Support movements that move to not put pregnant women behind bars. Find organizations locally that will offer support to mothers in this situation.
8. Offer the family support: offer to babysit, find car seats, clothes, bottles, or other things that they may not have for the child.
9. Look up local information on parental rights and send that information. Help to advocate for visitation and retention of custody if that is an issue.

10. Support comprehensive legislation around issues of pregnancy and postpartum for inmates' anti-shackling (anti-restraint is broader and even better to support) laws for pregnant and postpartum women as well as the abolition of medical isolation for women after delivery.

What the Prison Birth Project Needs:
- Financial Contributions!
- Committee members (even people from afar can join the research committee and help incarcerated women get the wide range of issues they need researched!)
- Grant writers and fierce fundraisers!
- People who want to put on fundraisers in their communities to help support the work we are doing!
- Journal-makers!
- Books on pregnancy, childbirth, addiction, and recovery
- Newborn baby clothes in good condition
- Food gift cards
- Childcare!

Organizing within an Anarcha-Feminist Childrearing Collective

CRAP! Collective (Child Rearing Against Patriarchy)

We demand a feminist upbringing for the next generation. We want to actively challenge the tirade of sexist racist capitalist classist homophobic transphobic ageist and ableist toys, media and literature produced for children; to empower and inspire the role of parenting caring and educating; and to combat patriarchy in all its forms within our children's lives. We would like to create networks to support and discuss feminist childrearing issues and push childrearing issues in feminist activist circles." —CRAP! first collective statement, 2008

CRAP! (Child Rearing Against Patriarchy) Collective arose out of a discussion group entitled "feminist childrearing," organized by three anarcha-feminist mothers, at a 2008 squatted feminist gathering in East London, England. A feminist childrearing revolution? Shouldn't take long, we thought!

As well as compiling zines, leading workshops, and writing articles for our blog and other publications, we have also made essential links and worked together with like-minded groups and collectives, parents, carers, and allies. These include pro-feminist men, people without children, activist and anarchist campaign groups, and feminist and childrearing allies internationally. We have also organised childcare and kidspaces at radical events, family blocs on demonstrations and actions, and been active within radical childcare collectives.

There are massive divergences between the spheres occupied and lived by those with and without caring responsibilities. Even within radical spaces or revolutionary groups, so often little attempt is made to include and encourage parents/carers and their children to attend. Within no time, non-parent/carer allies had mislabeled CRAP! Collective as the group of mothers who could provide childcare last-minute for their event. We often accepted, as we wanted each event to be as child-friendly as possible. But, after total burnout, we concluded that this was neither radical nor revolutionary. We want to push the boundaries surrounding attitudes towards childcare, mothers and kids in our radical communities, not do the babysitting!

Over the last few years, CRAP! Collective has organized, and participated in, many varied and essential actions and events. It has been an attempt at fusing our personal and political realities and visions. We have learnt a lot, usually the hard way. Non-parents/carers are crucial to the success of parent-led organising, so we've added suggestions to the lists below to help the inclusion of non-parents. It is important we share these experiences so that we don't continually reinvent the wheel when it comes to organising in a pro-kid way.

When organising a family bloc for a demo or a family-friendly action:

Prepare Early: Don't leave your placard painting until three hours before the demo starts. Sounds obvious, but it can be surprising what you can forget in all the excitement! Early preparation is essential to avoid stressing yourself and your kids out on the morning of the event. Give yourself plenty of time to get to meeting points and allow for nappy changes, nosebleeds, tantrums, and all the weird and wonderful things that go with bringing children anywhere. Fun and creative non-parent allies are needed to help make props before the event and liven up a flagging kidsbloc on the day.

Allocate Roles: Ensure that both an experienced first aider/street medic and a trusted legal observer will accompany the kidsbloc at all times. If your legal observer will be filming, always make a collective agreement with them before the event about whether the footage will be kept or destroyed afterwards (we have had a documentary filmmaker pose as an impartial legal observer, and now have no control over how his images will be used). A mainbloc-kidsbloc representative is needed to continually feedback crucial information whilst on the demo so nobody's left in the dark. We all should be aware of our rights and the general plan of the day, so as not to feel isolated. Ideally these important roles should be filled by a child-friendly but childless volunteer, so please offer your services.

Dynamics: Think about the placement of the kidsbloc in relation to the rest of the demo. Will you lead, remain at the tail-end, or disperse yourselves throughout? If it is likely to kick off at certain points, think about how you will deal with this collectively as a bloc. Should you involve children in this particular demo or arrange a separate child-friendly one? State your views/worries clearly, and emphasize that you will not allow children to be used as media-bait. Main bloc organizers, please talk openly about these options with a trusted representative of the kidsbloc in planning meetings.

Essential Supplies: Bring enticing snacks, energizing drinks, and always have bubble mixture to hand out! As well as being fun, masks and face paints also work well to disguise you and your kids from roving paparazzi/police cameras. Creative resources such as pavement chalks can be used en route as a kid-friendly action.

When organizing kidspaces at convergences, protest camps, or events:

Safe Spaces: The London G20 convergence center got violently raided by the cops (the police entered with guns drawn and forced everyone to lie on the floor). We sensibly had decided to have the kidspace in another building. Always formulate a collective Safer Spaces Policy and fully discuss media/comrade photography, and inform the rest of the event about your decisions (verbally and on easily visible posters). The main event organizers need to share important information with the kidspace crew prior to the event, adhere to the kidspace's policies, and offer help with written risk assessments/first aid kits, so that we can all make safe and informed decisions.

Emergency Contacts: Have a folder specifically for important information and ensure you write down parent/carer and emergency contact details, allergies, and other important information just in case. However, it is essential to immediately destroy this folder afterwards. We left these details in a squatted kidspace overnight only to return the next day to find the building (and therefore the kidspace information folder) had been reclaimed by the cops. We will never know if the police read the folder's information or threw it away immediately.

Start a Toy Bank: Toys that provide open-ended and imaginative play are the most successful, for example, dressing up, play-dough. Ask for people to donate old toys/materials, and arrange a suitable storage place so that you can build up a good selection for your collective, and other groups to use at later dates. Non-parents/carers are needed to help in the collecting, storage, transportation and upkeep of the toy bank.

Be Realistic: Recognize your limitations and don't take too much upon yourselves. The most important thing is to provide a vital service to the kids and parents/carers, not that you offer a first-class children's workshop extravaganza! Non-parent/carer allies—please do offer your workshops and time to the kidspace, but we rely on you to turn up and stick to what you've promised. However, in reality, kidspace schedules sometimes go amiss, so please be flexible if you are asked to lead the workshop at another time.

Kidspace vs. Crèche: Make it clear whether you are offering childcare (parents/carers can leave their kids with you) or a kidspace (where parents/carers can hang out and play with their kids). You only should offer to mind other people's kids if you know them well, have discussed what to do should certain scenarios occur, and are qualified and experienced enough to do so. However, you will always end up with some kids being sneakily dumped upon you for the day! So be clear that children are always their parents/carers' responsibility and have posters up saying so. Ensure also that individual workshops are publicised on programs as being "parent/carer and child friendly" or "not suitable for children" for those people who can't leave their kids in the crèche.

Daily Meetings: Take turns in representing the kidspace at every single site meeting, getting concrete offers of help there and then for that day. Put up a To Do list in the main area, the kidspace, and even the toilets! Make sure you encourage non-parents (of all genders) to sign up and involve themselves in the kidspace. It is also important to have a regular kidspace meeting after the main site meeting, feeding back vital information from the rest of the event to your crew, sharing feedback/ ideas and catching up on how everyone's doing/feeling. Good facilitation is needed for a quick and productive meeting, so non-parents are needed to facilitate (it's hard to focus on the topic in question when you're halfway through changing a runaway nappy!).

People Care: Kidspace crew organizers are usually those with children themselves. Imagine how exhausted you would be doing this job!

Non-parents: introduce yourselves, regularly visit the kidspace crew and offer help, make tea, get lunch or cover toilet/rest breaks. See what needs doing and do it! Lunch should always be offered first to the kidspace crew and children, then opened up to the rest of the event. Take care of your kidspace crew and your event will have a rockin' kidspace!

Raise Some Hell: Refuse to be subjugated into the dingy basement and demand a suitable kidspace area and facilities with easy buggy access. Child and family provisions should not be an afterthought but an integral part of every event. Ask non-parents to provide a kids' version of the adult workshops, so that the younger generation feel involved and respected for their participation. For example, at the Camp for Climate Action 2009, the "What Is Climate Change?" workshop was adapted for children and they got to perform at the camp closing gathering.

Childcare, childrearing, and child-friendly provisions should not be just defaulted as a mother's own issue. We see this as counter-revolutionary and a symptom of the sexism prevalent within radical movements. It is essential that people of all genders without children involve themselves in these areas. Communities, collectives, political groupings, and movements need to be thinking about and organizing decent childcare and creating inclusionary spaces where families are welcome and happy.

We are constantly coming up with great ideas, but have such precious little spare time. We have made some important gains, but even just surviving in this capitalist nightmare is difficult (never mind trying to self-organize around childcare). Both the negative and positive experiences we have had with non-parents whilst organizing within the Collective have reinforced our views that there is a real need to challenge such discriminatory behavior within our own circles as well as in wider society. Our original aims are therefore still our priority and we will carry on fighting for recognition of these issues. We will settle for nothing less than total revolution, and there will only be revolution if those with children are part of it.

An Open Letter to Movement Men
David Gilbert

February 17, 2010

To My Brothers in the Movement,

This open letter is a call, made both passionately and emphatically, for movement men to get fully involved in childcare. Childcare is one of the most demanding and most rewarding jobs in the world and is essential to advancing the struggle. I've been surprised to learn that in this day and age that responsibility still falls overwhelmingly on women. Men's failure in this regard is not only unfair but also hurts our movement since it is a major impediment to women's participation, to the full range of contribution they can make. But even more, if truth be told, this aloofness damages men the most because we cut ourselves off from the regular interactions that can enrich our lives in many ways. Children ask the questions that make us think more deeply about everything, exude the energy that buoys our spirits, embody the potential that gives us hope for the future.

It's for the children that we fight to make a better world. Brothers, it is way past due to get fully involved in childcare.

David Gilbert
(anti-imperialist political prisoner)

Men Running Childcare
London Pro-Feminist Men's Group

Some of us in the Pro-Feminist Men's Group work with children in various capacities already and we all share the conviction that pro-feminist men doing childcare is a great idea. It's one way we can support mothers and other carers (usually also women) and to facilitate feminist organising by giving parents and carers some free time to attend workshops, planning meetings, etc. It also shows that men can provide loving childcare and that raising kids isn't "women's work." It's also something that men's groups in the 1970s and '80s used to do to support the Women's Liberation movement. Childcare at political events continues to be underprovided today. Those of us that do work with kids also love it and have really enjoyed doing childcare in a political context.

For example, one member of the group recently helped run a kidspace on Raven's Ait (an island in the Thames near Surbiton) during the G20 protests. A few of us ran the crèche/playroom at the Gender, Race and Class conference at SOAS in February 2009 and a couple of us also ran a smaller crèche during a feminist planning meeting back in the summer. We're planning to continue this work in various forms (Feminism in London Conference in 2010 for one) and aim to work closely with the CRAP! Collective (Child Rearing Against Patriarchy) to develop further links with parents and carers who want to make sure that they and their kids are not excluded from political events.

Below is a report about the recent kidspace on the island, written by one of the CRAP! Collective members, who was also one of the organisers.

The kidspace and childcare cooperative was organised by the CRAP! Collective, London Pro-Feminist Men's Group, the Global Mutiny Network and the community of Ravens Ait Island.

Raven's Ait is a squatted island on the River Thames near Surbiton, South London. This artificially made island, which is actually still common land, is steeped in political history, although more recently has been used for weddings and corporate events. The present occupants are creating an amazing peaceful space for community, an eco-conference centre, permaculture gardens and workshops on sustainability and environmental issues.

Raven's Ait was the perfect place for the kidspace. We had a large indoor playroom with views of the river and passing boats, and a stunning grass lawn for the kids to run around on and climb trees. We had loads of fun playing games and doing forest-school inspired crafts, such as making dream catchers/spiders webs, nature crowns, tipis, parachute games, football, twister, a mini rock concert, lots of drawing and painting, Spanish singing, picnics and even played croquet on the lawn, dahling! Being at Raven's Ait also gave the children a chance to experience communal living and working, in a safe space, away from the noise of the city and the police brutality during the G20 protests.

Many actions and demos can easily be made more welcoming for children and their carers to participate in and we would encourage this. However, in respect to the G20 protests, we made the decision that it was too unpredictable and heavy for our children to attend and, looking back, we feel we made the right decision organising the kidspace away from the action.

Mainstream society is not very welcoming to parents, carers, and children; I feel that often activism isn't either. Capitalism places no value, monetary or otherwise, on the work parents do, and patriarchy designates it as women's work. As activists we need to challenge these notions. We need to ensure that as much value is placed on the role of childcare as is placed on all other aspects of organising actions, demos, meetings, workshops, etc. We also need to challenge the sexist notion that women should be looking after the children by ensuring that more men are given childcare roles. Paid childcare is very expensive; most of us can't afford to pay for it to go to meetings or do actions, so if childcare isn't provided and children aren't welcome at meetings, then we just can't go. Even if childcare can't be arranged, then we should at least think about enabling children to attend with their parents/carers.

This is an appeal for all those organising in the UK at the moment to ensure that your organising facilitates parents, carers, and children attending and getting involved.

Don't leave your friends behind!

Continuing the Struggle: Lessons Learned from Mothers and Children in Zapatista Communities

Victoria Law

But it is not just the Zapatista villages that have grown—the EZLN has also grown. Because what has happened during this time is that new generations have renewed our entire organization. They have added new strength. The comandantes and comandantas who were in their maturity at the beginning of the uprising in 1994 now have the wisdom they gained in the war and in the twelve years of dialogue with thousands of men and women from throughout the world. The members of the CCRI, the Zapatista political-organizational leadership, is now counseling and directing the new ones who are entering our struggle, as well as those who are holding leadership positions. For some time now the "committees" (which is what we call them) have been preparing an entire new genera-tion of comandantes and comandantas who, following a period of in-struction and testing, are beginning to learn the work of organizational leadership and to discharge their duties. And it also so happens that our insurgents, insurgentas, militants, local and regional responsables, as well as support bases, who were youngsters at the beginning of the uprising, are now mature men and women, combat veterans and natural leaders in their units and communities. And those who were children in that January of '94 are now young people who have grown up in the re-sistance, and they have been trained in the rebel dignity lifted up by their elders throughout these twelve years of war. These young people have a political, technical and cultural training that we who began the Zapatista movement did not have. This youth is now, more and more, sustaining our troops as well as leadership positions in the organization. —from the Sixth Declaration of the Selva Lacandona[1]

---

1. On January 1, 1994, an army of indigenous people surprised the Mexican government and the world with several armed uprisings in Mexico's southernmost state of Chiapas. The EZLN (Ejército Zapatista de Liberación Nacional or Zapatistas) demanded land, freedom, and the rights to employment, housing, food, health, education, self-determination, democracy, justice, and peace. Since the uprising, the EZLN has reclaimed several large stretches of land, transforming them

I had originally been inspired to go to the First Zapatista Women's *Encuentro* in 2007 by the call to volunteer at the Non-Conformist Cultural Center. Recognizing that a convening of women required a safe (and fun!) place for them to leave their children while they attended meetings, plenaries and workshops, volunteers from a solidarity group put a call out for people around the world to help put together not just childcare, but a Non-Conformist Cultural Center where activities would reflect the plenaries and sessions that their mothers were participating in.

As a mother who pushes for the social justice movement to support the parents and children in the struggle, I was excited. For the past year and a half, I had attended (predominantly white) anarchist and feminist events to present "Don't Leave Your Friends Behind." My daughter Siu Loong, at ages five and six, accompanied me and had a chance to experience each event's childcare (or lack thereof). At some, such as the Children's Social Forum at the 2007 United States Social Forum (USSF), she had participated in activities reflecting the social justice themes of the day, discussing concepts such as gentrification, war, and gender in ways that she, and other children her age, could grasp.

Reading about the plan for a Non-Conformist Cultural Center, I was intrigued. What would radical childcare in a Zapatista community look like?

Then I got a call from Terry, a mother I had roomed with at the 2007 USSF. She and her now-three-year-old daughter Pi were members of a delegation of women of color (and white allies) who were going to the *encuentro*. Was I interested in joining? My answer was an unequivocal Yes![2]

I didn't find the Non-Cultural Conformist Center until the second day of the three-day *encuentro*. It was far from the center of the community where the plenary sessions and other activities were taking place. A woman and several boys were painting a mural on the cinderblock façade of the school. Other boys raced around hitting each other with empty plastic bottles, apparently a favorite game among children in the *campo*. There were eight childcare providers and eight little boys. The man I spoke to looked at Pi and said, "There aren't any girls here."

"Why not?" we asked.

---

into liberated Zapatista communities that are run independently of the Mexican government.

2. My daughter Siu Loong chose to go to her grandparents' house for their annual Christmas celebration.

He shrugged. "Maybe they are busy working."

Only much later did I begin to realize that the concept of orga-nized childcare—of separating children from the adult activities—is a Western capitalist concept. In other cultures, children are integrated into daily life, not shunted into a corner or separate room far from grown-up eyes and ears. The Zapatistas didn't need the kind of childcare usually expected by those of us north of the border. They incorporated their children into the struggle, teaching not only with stories and words but also by example. After all, the children (and their children and their chil-dren's children) are who the struggle is ultimately for. To emphasize this point, many of the T-shirts and bags sold during the *encuentro* depicted small children growing out of cornstalks.

Throughout the plenary sessions, children ran in and out of the au-ditorium to see and sit with their mothers or to be hugged before dash-ing off to resume playing outside. Babies sometimes cried, but no one took much notice and, unlike meetings and events in the north, no one even dared suggest that the mother leave. Masked girls sat beside their mothers, listening to the stories of what their lives might have looked like had they not been born into the movement.

"Before, only the men and boys could have fun," Comandanta Rosalinda said on the first day. "Girls had to take care of the babies and never had time to go to school or even to play."

Having heard stories from their parents and grandparents, children, particularly the girls, understand the significance of what they now have. Marina stood before thousands of women from around the world and, in the clear words of a girl just about to turn nine, stated what the revo-lution means to her:

> I want to tell you about my life. I study in an autonomous Zapatista school because I have rights. My parents respect my right to dance, to sing, to have fun. In my autonomous school, sometimes we don't have school supplies and we don't ask the government because we are part of the resistance. My father works in his fields and sells his harvest so that we have money to buy my school supplies. We are Zapatistas and we don't take crumbs from the government. I am very proud to be a Zapatista; we won't be discouraged because we are used to resisting.

That evening, a woman from our delegation wondered aloud about the girl's speech: could a nine-year-old really have come up with these words and sentiments on her own?

Raising a child of my own in the struggle and having seen how her older peers talk and think, I defended the girl's sincerity. When children are taught and included from an early age, they absorb these teachings. They ask questions about experiences and realities. If their questions aren't dismissed or silenced, their understanding and consciousness grows.

Mothers both in and out of the Zapatista movement are the primary teachers of their children. For many women, the Zapatistas were the first to encourage them to think, question and learn: "Before the EZLN, we [the mothers] didn't have this education. We didn't know that we could fight a just fight for the well-being of our children. We dedicated ourselves to working in our homes and in the homes of the landowners. Our children were raised like animals. We didn't educate our children [before] because we didn't know these things. The landowners didn't teach us so they could keep us as workers," said Maribel, a Zapatista mother.

Integrating mothers has been crucial to continuing the struggle. This sentiment was repeated again and again as women from the different *caracoles* spoke about their experiences:[3]

"As mothers, we set examples for our children," stated Elizabeth, a mother from La Realidad. "We teach them that unless you fight, you are fucked. As mothers, we show by example, by taking on responsibilities and participation in the EZLN, in the region, in the CCRI. We teach our children not to contaminate the earth with chemicals so that it will continue to provide for us and for future generations."

"When our children are small, we talk to them about what they'd like to do when they are big," stated Elena, a mother from Oventic. "We talk about options in the military, in the community, and in doing political work. We tell them that they have the same rights as the *Ladrones* [light-skinned landowners]. We talk about the resistance and why we resist. We teach them why we don't receive help from the bad government."

Some women spoke about the difficulties of actively participating in the struggle. Some husbands do not understand the importance of

---

3. Each autonomous region is governed by a caracol (literally "snailshell," but in actuality each region's center of "good government.") According to Mayan legend, the gods who made the world did not have time to finish the sky. Four gods placed themselves at the four corners of the earth to hold the sky in place. They often became distracted, however, and so one god held watch, carrying a caracol (or conch shell) to awake the others if evil fell on the earth. This god subsequently taught men and women how to use the caracol to alert others to evil in the world.

women's participation, fearing that if their wives are active in the community, the work at home is left undone. Other husbands agree to their wives' public participation provided that they continue do all of the housework and childcare.

Zapatista mothers are actively raising the next generation to combat these entrenched oppressions and gender expectations: "We teach the boys housework so that when they are bigger they can help. This creates a sense of equality between boys and girls. We teach [all our children] to defend ourselves and our community when the army comes in to try to evict us," said Elena.

Gabriella, another mother from Oventic, explained that, without the participation of the mothers, the struggle falters: "Sometimes mothers will say they can't participate because they don't understand the importance of their participation. Some women do not want to send their children to the autonomous school because there is so much responsibility at home and they don't understand the concept of collectivism."

For the mothers who do participate in the struggle, their children—both boys and girls—learn from their examples. They teach their children by modeling what women's participation looks like and show them how this is important.

The lessons for us visitors should not be that our communities are relieved of the responsibility of providing childcare or otherwise supporting the specific needs of mothers and children. Rather, we have witnessed how the Zapatistas incorporate children into their struggle, how they include mothers and children rather than shunting them into a corner or onto the outskirts. And, fourteen years after the uprising, we see that those who were small children in 1994, who grew up in the movement, now enter and continue the struggle for dignity and liberty.

Now, when we return home to organize ourselves, we need to find a way to do the same in our own communities and movements.

Five

LISTS, LESSONS, AND CONCRETE TIPS FOR SUPPORTING CHILDREN AND CAREGIVERS

We see childcare as a political act. The founders of the Childcare Collective were also inspired by the vision of "Sisters at the Center"—the idea, developed by the School of Unity and Liberation (SOUL), that working class women of color need to be at the center our movements, in terms of analysis, issues, and leadership. The Childcare Collective aims to support this vision by providing childcare so that working class women of color and immigrants could continue building movements that only they can lead. The simple act of providing childcare allows individuals to be involved in organizing and community-building without facing the restraints of finding reliable and affordable childcare.
— "An Interview with the Bay Area Childcare Collective," *Left Turn* (April 2007)

In this section we offer practical checklists for those who want to:

• support families,
• create child-inclusive spaces at events,
• organize childcare and kids' activities.

Some of these suggestions echo those made in earlier essays; we provide them here in easy-to-read format.

We also encourage readers to be inspired by these lists—as well as the issues they don't see listed—to make their own lists. Reach out to others: ask for help, and ask how you can help. We need to communicate with each other in order to work on concrete ways we can make a difference. Sharing (and creating!) lists, lessons, and tips can help in this work.

Tips on How to Support Your Friend During Pregnancy
Jessica Hoffmann

- Clean the litter box. There's a parasite in cat feces that can be harmful to pregnant women, so offer to take this chore off your pregnant loved one's to-do list.
- Learn about pregnancy and childbirth. Your pregnant loved one is going through something big, and, like with anything in life, it feels good when people you're in close relationships with care enough to educate themselves about what you're going through.
- Understand that at different points in pregnancy, your loved one may be more tired than usual or emotional in a different way from usual. Don't pathologize it or make assumptions about what they can or can't do, but be sensitive to the fact that they are going through real physical and emotional changes.
- Listen. As with anything, listen to people you love. Pregnancy isn't the same for everyone, so while it's great to educate yourself about it from books, movies, and other resources, it's also important to listen to how it feels for your loved one in particular.
- If you're asked to be a birth partner, educate yourself about childbirth, follow the pregnant/birthing person's lead, and be sure to take care of yourself so that you have the strength and balance to be a good support during an important and sometimes challenging moment.
- Be curious but not intrusive. Show curiosity and interest in your loved one's pregnancy, but don't assume it's okay to touch their belly, offer parenting advice, or anything else without checking in or being invited. As with anything, consent matters.
- Ask what your pregnant loved one could use help with and help where/how you can. Maybe they need help lifting big things, or picking things up off the floor once their belly gets very big, or maybe they could use moral support at doctor's visits or in dealing with their excitement/nerves/etc. about being a parent. Don't as-

sume what they need, as everyone is different, but listen, ask, and offer the kinds of help you can give.

- Talk about childbirth preferences and choices with your loved one if they want to talk about this. Recognize that it's both a political and a personal topic and be sensitive to talking in a way that's helpful/ illuminating/supportive but not judgmental. These are big, loaded choices.

Taking Care of Your Friends Postpartum
Clayton Dewey

Having a baby is one of the biggest life changers people experience. It's an exciting time and amazing to suddenly have a brand new baby in your arms. At the same time, the move from babyless to babyful (or from one to two, two to three, etc.) can be a sudden and drastic change with definite challenges. As a friend, it's really great to be there for the joys of a new baby and to help with the difficulties that come with being a new parent.

When we had our kids, some of the smallest gestures were just the thing to keep our sanity level. Having a new baby can be really hard and sometimes just knowing that other people understand that this is a big deal goes a long way. Here's what our friends and family did for us during those first few weeks with baby.

- Brought over food
- Cleaned our house so we could spend more time with the baby and relax
- Sent cards
- Called us
- Brought us clothes or gifts (see below for ideas)
- Visited us
- Watched the kids so we could go on a date (with tiny baby in tote)
- Shared stories of being new parents
- Still invited us to shows and events (but let us know further ahead of time so we could plan accordingly)
- Planned party for people to see the baby
- Were there to listen to the happy, the sad, and the troubling

Gift Ideas
- Screenprinted onesies, blankies, and other baby paraphernalia
- DIY shirts or other clothing items

- Kid/parent zines or magazines
- Dumpstered or thriftstore toys or clothes (washed before giving to us)
- Massage
- Cloth diapers (they're expensive up front so helping buy them is a great way to help a family out)

Babyproofing for Punks
Clayton Dewey

It's always interesting to walk into a collective house or punk house that proudly has a "This is a Safe Space" sign nailed to the wall, while the house is amazingly dirty and littered with unsafe objects. Oftentimes, kids are not worked into the equation of what makes a space safe. Of course, we could also analyze how a space that is largely dirty and unkempt might feel unsafe or off-putting to someone who has been working hard to move out of situations like that, especially if the house is occupied by those benefitting from class privilege who are willing to live in squalor. But that's another topic.

Here we are talking about creating safe spaces for kids, specifically babies and toddlers who are visiting.

An Honest Assessment

You and your housemates need to be honest. Many anarchist houses do have lower standards of cleanliness. Be realistic about what you are willing to do. Be clear and honest to parents about that as well. If you really can't get your house to a safe level for a toddler, be real about that. It might suck for us parents to hear that, but it's better than being dishonest about it or dropping the ball once we come over.

Designating a Kid-Safe Space

Depending on your living situation, it might feel overwhelming to make your house okay for kids to crawl around in. Have no fear! There are ways to make your house safe for kids without scrubbing and sweeping all day.

If you are pressed for time or just cannot maintain a decent degree of cleanliness, then pick one room and make it baby-friendly. Even if the rest of the house remains in its splendor of filth, being able to offer up a sanctuary for parents and kid is often very welcome.

You can take this concept as far as you'd like. Maybe pick a few rooms (common rooms are the best) or the whole first floor. When it's nice outside, offer up the backyard. If your place is overwhelmingly kid unsafe, start small with a certain area and go from there.

Start with the Most Life-Threatening
- Pick up glass bottles, especially the broken ones!
- Lock up or put up high any toxic or hazardous chemicals and cleaners (If you have a graywater toilet, figure out a way to keep the kids out of the bathroom).
- Cover electrical outlets; duct tape will do!
- Either keep houseplants up high, or make sure you know what they are and that they aren't harmful if bitten or eaten.

Pretend to Be a Baby
Get a toilet paper tube, get on your hands and knees and start crawling around. Anything that can fit inside that cardboard tube needs to be put away; removing the chokeable objects is key. You can get all your friends to do it with you!

While you're down there, try pulling things like bookshelves, your record player, etc. Babies like to climb up things and the thought of that massive bookshelf of zines and radical literature crashing down is pretty terrifying.

Cleaning
It's your call as to how dirty the floor is. If it was pretty gross crawling around, then you should probably sweep/mop/vacuum. When our kid was a baby, we helped prep for Food Not Bombs. After just a few minutes, his knees and hands were pitch black with soot and nastiness.

If you intend for your house to be a main staple of entertainment for kids, here are some other things you can do to kick your place up to super safedom:

- Shorten drapery and blind cords.
- Keep bottles of Ipecac and activated charcoal in your home in case of poisoning (but don't use it unless you've got the go-ahead by someone who knows the human body well).
- Place screened barriers around fireplaces, radiators, and portable space heaters.
- Install hardware-mounted safety gates at the top and bottom of

stairways with two or more steps.
- Keep appliance cords wrapped short so children cannot pull coffeemakers, toasters, and other appliances.

For more ideas, you can visit http://www.safekids.org.

If, after reading this article, you don't think your house can create a kid-safe space, think about other ways you might be able to support your parent and kid friends: maybe there's a cool park nearby where you can spend time with them, or maybe you have a certain skill you can share with the kiddos in a child-safe location. Brainstorm with the parents and kids to see how you can contribute and be an ally outside of your home, if not in your home.

Supporting Your Friend Who Lost Their Newborn Infant
Mikaela Shafer

When I lost my daughter, I felt very alone. I was young, far from all my close friends, and completely unprepared for such a loss. I have written down some steps I wish I had the courage to ask my friends to take then. Do read and take them in: your friends may need you one day.

Sit, Listen, and Cry
Don't be afraid of me. Hug me for a long time. Listen and cry with me. Say, "I'm so fucking sorry." I need to know you care.

Food, Health, and Laughter
Make me dinner and make sure I'm okay and taking care of myself. Tell me I'm strong. Tell me stories of way back when we were young and full of adventure. I need smiles and I need soup.

Rituals and Cleansing
Help me honor her. Help me build a fire, scream into the wind, beg the gods for answers. Hold my hand as I built an altar. Tell me you'll always be there for me.

Into the Night
It can get hard to go out. I fear people asking me what happened and if I'm okay. Be there. Encourage me to dress up. Be my friend and my gang. Tell me you have my back.

Memorials and Ice Cream
A year or two or more have passed and I still need you. Come over when the date rolls around and tell me I'm doing amazing. Howl at the moon, light candles, or make dinner. Bring over a movie and ice cream and hold my hand when I am reminded of my baby and start to cry. Remind me of all the good in my life and never let me forget.

Concrete Things You Can Do to Support Parents and Children in Your Scene:
Suggestions Brainstormed at La Rivolta!, an Anarcha-Feminist Conference in Boston, 2006

Give children attention. Say something to them. Just be your true self, whatever you are thinking, they are open to that. Children act better when they get attention. At the beginning of a meeting, if a group gives the children some attention, they are often happier and better behaved for the rest of the meeting.

Develop childcare as an ongoing relationship with a child. It takes some time to get to know a child before they are comfortable with you away from their parents.

Offer a slot of time to spend time with a child on a weekly basis.

Integrate children and adults. It's more pleasant to watch children with other adults to talk to; it's more pleasant for the children to see adults enjoying each other and not feeling like a burden to them.

Include children in the planning of any activity.

Doing something child-friendly? Ask a kid if they want to come along. (Lizxnn took Siu Loong for Critical Mass rides for three years and she loved it.) Children can benefit from being part of activities their parents don't do and parents can benefit from the time to themselves.

If a baby is crying and needs to be held, and the parent has their hands busy, offer to hold the baby.

If a child is making a disturbance, offer to go outside with the kid so the parent doesn't have to leave the event.

Meet parents at their level. Visit them at home or wherever their spaces are. Let parents talk about being parents.

Acknowledge children. Don't treat them as if they are invisible.

At meetings and events that we wish to make child-friendly, announce that we are okay with children making noise, that we can talk over them, and that we value mothers and children sticking around. This announcement can help put mothers at ease.

Give parents and children a smile!

When providing childcare at political events (and every event should have childcare!):

- Visit the children and childcare providers in daycare. Childcare providers can feel isolated from others at the event. Have a cup of tea with them! (suggested by Siu Loong, age five)
- Parents with different aged children have different needs. Parents with younger children or children who aren't comfortable leaving their parents yet would benefit from childcare that was in the same room. Parents with older and more independent children benefit from having them in a different room. Either way, childcare must be accessible.
- Parents need to give more input to the childcare providers about their and their children's needs during the planning of the event for the childcare provider(s) to better support them. At the very least, tell them you are coming and the age of your child/ren.
- It's comforting for parents to know that childcare is available, even if they don't use it.

And contemplate:

- How much work and how consuming it is being a parent, twenty-four/seven. In the beginning years, it's hard to even think straight; one is still adjusting to being a parent and young children's needs are very intensive.
- That radical parents often don't fit in at mainstream places, like their children's schools. Think about how it might feel to go to an anarchist/radical gathering and not feel supported by their own culture.

Lessons from Planning Radical Childcare
China Martens

I first planned childcare at the 2006 Radical Mid-Atlantic Bookfair, after I went to a meeting to recommend that they offer childcare. I never imagined that I would wind up being the one to organize it, but they didn't have anyone else![1]

Kidz Corner was a huge success, but coordinating it was a lot of work. I realized that the next goal would be to collectivize the organizing work so that the responsibility didn't fall on only one person. A few years later, I had the opportunity to collaborate with Kidz City, the childcare component of the 2009 City From Below conference. It inspired us (Harriet Moon Smith, Sine Hwang Jensen, and myself) to stay together even after the event was over, keeping "Kidz City" as the name of our radical childcare collective. While we've organized childcare at numerous events since then, Kidz City is still learning how to work together and grow.[2]

Lessons learned so far:

- Start planning for childcare at the beginning of the event planning, not at the last minute! For Kidz City, we request a month's notice for an event lasting a few hours; three to four months' notice for a longer event; and five to six months' notice for organizing at a three-day conference.

---

1. I had just returned home inspired by the amazing childcare at the 2006 Montreal Anarchist Bookfair where we had given a Don't Leave Your Friends Behind workshop. I guess I listened to my own talk about the importance of providing childcare and realized it could apply to myself, now that my arms were free and my daughter was eighteen.

2. Kidz City Baltimore is an all-volunteer anarcha-feminist collective dedicated to increasing access and support for parents, children, and caregivers in social justice organizing and at events. We partner with others to organize creative space, care, and programming for children. We see childcare as a form of activism and one part of creating a more just world (http://kidzcitybaltimore.blogspot.com/).

- Embedding in the larger event is important. For Kidz Corner, being part of the larger event meant that we could draw from a larger pool of volunteers, have food provided and space made available. Security volunteers were aware of children; we discussed their concerns about safety and how to talk to children (because it was something that they brought up. You will likely have your own issues to address with working with your own larger event).
- Put "childcare available" on all flyers. Ask the larger event to put "childcare available" on their flyers, websites, and other outreach material so people know to bring kids. Every time the event is mentioned, the kidz program (whether childcare, space, or events) should be mentioned too!
- You may want to write a small manifesto about what you are doing and why childcare is important. You can then retool it down the road for different purposes (flyers, blogs, programs, interviews).
- Space for childcare must be accessible and close to the main activities, the more visible the better! Try not to get marginalized by being assigned the space in the far far back or basement. If that's all you can get cuz space is tight, cheer it up! Decorate with inspirational art, make the space attractive and friendly. For Kidz Corner, we made a banner together. My daughter outlined the words, and kids and volunteers colored it in. Tour the space so you can see what it needs. Also, think about other spaces, like outdoor space.
- Prioritize the care of the young, even if there aren't many children this time. Creating a space is a great practice for next time. No matter how many kids come, it's important! Sometimes the room can be empty, then suddenly fill up. Children and caretakers can also use this space to play, to chill out from the larger event, and to meet others.
- Don't let people store other stuff in the kids' space. It's not safe. For instance, when free food was stored in the Kidz Corner, people coming in to get food didn't look out for the kids underfoot. Someone also dropped a container; glass fell near a baby's head and all over the ground. People will also want to come and use your space to organize for their workshops while ignoring the children around them. Simply tell space-seekers that the room is prioritized for children and they cannot use it.
- Planning meetings need to be accessible to parents. I think it's ideal for an organizer to be able to coordinate between radical parents

and the childfree radical community. Ask local parents, groups and those who might attend: How can you support them? Ask the children too! Get ideas from parents and kids, create dialogue with radical parents and radical community, pull in all the resources you can.

• *But* don't ask the parents to do childcare (although parents' participation should be welcome). Parents always have to do childcare. This is a service to those whose children are old/comfortable enough to be left so that parents can go to a workshop, read, or participate without their attention being divided. It is also a chance for those without children of their own to participate with children.

• Create a scheduling volunteer sheet with contact numbers. Create a separate sign-in sheet with name, age, parents' contact information, and any relevant thing you need to know. Make sure everyone signs in and out. Have sticker nametags.

• Have at least three volunteers for each two to three hour shift, so that there are at least two volunteers in the room at all times. You may need more depending on how many children are coming and their ages. Volunteers should be screened; if you signed them up, you should know who they are. Always try to pair up a more experienced person with a less experienced one.

• Take care of the childcare volunteers. No one should ever be left alone or overburdened. Having one or two people to keep an eye on the room for the day creates consistency. Make sure these people can have a few substantial breaks throughout the day (or even take a long lunch off or leave early for the day). It's even better to create a collective organizing team and have the day divided up with a few different bottom-liners (childcare coordinators).

• Radical childcare means respectful radical programming for the kids. Think about how the theme of the larger event can apply to children and vice versa. Use the values of the event in developing the children's programming and advocate for children and caretakers within the larger organization. Ask presenters if they want to do a mini-workshop for the kids.

• Make different levels of ways for volunteers to be involved, from childcare responsibilities to just coming in and playing. The more energy the better! Childcare is a high-need activity and the more the volunteers are supported, the more they can provide the most respectful attention to the children. Event childcare is not like a normal childcare situation. Everyone is new and getting to know each other and the energy of the room can change quickly. You need to create a strong infrastructure to support positive all-ages interaction and spontaneity.

• Take care of the kids. Make sure each child is attended to and the environment is safe.

• Food! Have food, drink, and cleanup supplies in the room. Have a plan for mealtime.

• Plan kinetic activities as well as arts and crafts and space for quiet time. Is there a playground nearby? Trees to climb? A sidewalk that you can play hopscotch on? Kids need to get physical, some more than others.

• Keep in mind that sometimes there is a need for a one-on-one person for really small children or for children with special needs. It helps if there is a possibility for parents to be able to set up one-on-one childcare before they arrive. (Suggested by Amy Hamilton in *Moving towards a Family-Friendly Radical Movement*)

• If there are not enough childcare volunteers or if you don't feel comfortable with providing childcare, you can at least set up a space for children and adults to gather, play, interact, and organize their own childcare swaps if they like.

• Plan to have people you can call for back-up childcare and also what you would do in case of an emergency. For Kidz Corner, I could call security if I had a problem (they also knew CPR). I also had phone numbers for parents and tablers who would come and help if I needed them.

• The DC Radical Childcare Collective has a rule that two volunteers always accompany a child to the bathroom.[3] That sounds like a good idea for safety. We sometimes visit the bathroom as a group and use the "buddy" system when walking together to a different space.

• You grow as you go. The first year that we had childcare at an anarchist event in Baltimore, I talked to people a lot about why and how. The second year was a fantastic experience with every community resource at my fingertips.

• Be accountable. Do what you say! I have seen flyers for events say-

---

3. The DC Childcare Collective has been providing childcare to parents involved in social justice activism in DC since the summer of 2005. The Collective came together at the suggestion of community organizers working on campaigns involving tenant's rights, privatization of public spaces in DC, and affordable, high-quality childcare for all. http://dcchildcarecollective.org.

ing that childcare is available, but then the childcare people don't show up or childcare is a mess and unsafe. Parents and caregivers are counting on you. Strong structure can take different levels of commitment and personality, but the main people who sign up really do need to be there, or (because life happens!) to call in as soon as possible to inform others and help find a replacement.

- Have fun with it! Inspiration makes things better.
- Remember that radical childcare is a radical tactic: by turning the system upside down, and learning how to work together to support everyone's rights, we include the young in the change we want to see now.

Radical Childcare Collective Start-Up Notes
Amariah Love/Kelli's Childcare Collective of Atlanta

What Brought Me to This Work
I have seen firsthand what the United States, its values, and its laws will do to poor single mothers. My mother was thrown into jail, into debt, into depression, into homelessness, and into unemployment because she was poor, had no community, no family support, and only a high school education. She was one of the millions who qualified for welfare but could never get it. She was reprimanded in court by a judge who did not know her for her bad parenting, regardless of the facts of her actual mothering. She killed herself because she saw no way out. If she had had a community—a group of people who paid attention to what she was going through and what her needs were and provided her with what she needed to survive—she would still be here. Mothers need support. Children need to have an established sense of community from a young age so that they carry those values throughout their lives. This issue is incredibly personal and important to me.

Planning Your First Meeting
It's important to have a pre-planned agenda. At the first meeting of Kelli's Childcare Collective Atlanta (KCCA), I created a presentation to get folks at the meeting talking about why radical childcare is so important. I also made copies of the sheet I typed so folks could have something to look at.

I created flyers and a Facebook event to get the word out. I invited people and made phone calls to everyone I knew who might be interested during the week before the meeting and on the day of the meeting. We had a very good turnout—about twelve people, two of whom brought their kids. We met at a comrade's home that had a spacious living room. The meeting lasted about two hours, with a break in the middle.

We had an excellent discussion about capitalism, how it affects families, and what it means for childcare. **I think it's also important** to put a time limit on such discussions. As fun and useful as they are, you want to come away from your meeting having taken next steps towards becoming a functional resource in your community. Have an agenda pre-determined to either type up and hand out or write on a big sheet of paper or whiteboard. In future meetings, it might make more sense to have agendas developed more organically by the folks present, but I think that at a first meeting it makes everyone's jobs easier if you have one pre-determined.

Next Steps

The most difficult part of starting a collective is organizing volunteers and building a reputation so that organizations in your community start coming to you when they need care. At the first meeting, it's important to figure out people's schedules, how to get in contact with them, and what kind of capacity you currently have for actually providing childcare. If an organization were to call you tomorrow and say, we have a meeting at 6 p.m. next Thursday, can y'all provide childcare, what would you need in order to make that happen?

For starters, you need:

• Volunteers who know where the space is, how long the meeting is, and what they are expected to do
• Toys and games (if the space you are going to does not provide them. Even if they do, it is still good to have your own)
• A person who is bottom-lining the event, i.e., is responsible for making sure the childcare happens and keeping in touch with the organization's contact person

At least for KCCA, the first few months were mostly the same four or five folks showing up to care gigs. What really helped us out was connecting with a well-connected organization in our area and partnering with them so that we were providing care for their ongoing meetings twice a month. This was within our capacity; it gave us a chance to network with other organizers and to build a reputation with that organization, who later recommended us to other organizations.

Ask folks at your meeting if there are any ideas for initial partnerships y'all could take on to build a foundation for your organizing.

Our First Experience

Our first childcare experience was at the first Georgia Students for Higher Public Education summer conference. This event went really well. I kept a notebook for KCCA-related stuff and created a chart to sign people up for shifts at the conference, as it was an all-day event. I signed about six people up for two-and-a-half-hour shifts, and personally committed to being there early in the morning to get everything set up and staying all day. We had a good turnout of kids, about six throughout the day, and everybody who signed up for a childcare shift showed up. At this event, the childcare space was a good five-to-ten-minute walk from certain parts of the conference. A mother who attended suggested that we try and communicate with the organizers that, for future events, the childcare space should be closer to the meeting space. I also wish that I had not committed to being on duty for the entire day, but at this point, I felt the need to supervise everything to make sure it ran smoothly and did not think to ask someone else to take on this role. Still, parents told us that they were more than satisfied with the childcare, that they were grateful because it made the conference more accessible to them, and that they were delighted to return to the childcare space to see smiles on their children's faces!

Nuts and Bolts of Childcare Organizing

There is so much need! You will likely find very quickly that there is a huge need for progressive childcare in your area. After only a year and a half of organizing, KCCA has four organizational partners for whom we provide care on a regular basis. We also have worked with around fifteen other organizations in Atlanta for various events. We have also worked with organizers in Athens to start a sister branch in that city to meet the needs of progressive organizations there, notably Freedom University. We get calls and e-mails several times a month from organizations we have and haven't worked with that are interested in our services. We are currently providing trainings and childcare for Occupy Atlanta. We have conducted upwards of twenty new volunteer trainings and a handful of organizer trainings.

Thanks to the time, effort, and dedication of many different folks from many different walks of life, we have created a structure for the collective that helps us efficiently coordinate everything. Over time, we came to decide some guiding rules for the collective. Our ability to provide quality childcare and to reach out to as many potential volunteers as possible always come first: we believe rules are not meant to be followed at the expense of acting rationally. So of course, we take our guidelines seriously, but are not opposed to being flexible when required. Importantly, we are always evolving and learning. I am sure that, in a year, things will look different! This is only the model we use now, but so far it has worked wonderfully. I hope some of this will be helpful to others trying to figure out what kind of structure works well for their community's needs.

How We Do It

Volunteers must attend a New Volunteer Orientation within their first few weeks of volunteering with us. These trainings get everybody on the same page about KCCA's policies, procedures, and conduct expectations for volunteers during childcare. At the beginning of the orientation, participants fill out a questionnaire designed to get them thinking about the intersections of race, class, and gender, and what they have to do with childcare activism. We then have a discussion about these issues and talk about KCCA's work and how we see ourselves situated in the broader movement. Following this discussion, we go over the policies, procedures, and so on. We also talk about why we decided to avoid non-profit status and about our criteria for partners. We have several role-plays scattered throughout this section to help emphasize some of the more important policies. At the end of the orientation, participants sign a volunteer agreement form. All of these documents (questionnaire, curriculum, and agreement form) are online at http://www.kccatl.com/documents.

Here are a few of the more important policies that you might find useful in figuring out how to create your own systems of accountability and organizational structure:

Sign In/Out Procedures: We are very strict about this procedure. We have sign in/out forms that ask for the names of the parent and child, the time they are dropped off and picked up, what allergies they have, whether there are any diet restrictions, and a contact number. We also have medical authorization forms that give us explicit permission to call an ambulance should an emergency happen. We tell our volunteers that it is mandatory for every parent to sign their child in and fill out a medical authorization form for each child. We keep the filled-out forms in a binder all together so that parents only have to fill it out once. Our volunteers are taught to let parents know that without being signed-in and having a medical form filled out, we cannot take responsibility for their children, no matter how close the event/meeting space is or how short the amount of time is that the child will be with us. This allows us to keep careful track of who we are responsible for at any given time and helps with liability issues as well.

Not Being Alone Policy: Our policy on being alone with children is also usually strict. In an effort to make sure that volunteers are held accountable and covered in case something bad happens that is out of their control, we do not allow KCCA volunteers to be alone with children at any time. We always make sure that at least two volunteers are on duty at all times. We tell our volunteers in the training that if they show up and no other volunteers are there for whatever reason, they need to contact their bottom-liner (childcare coordinator) and see if they can find another volunteer. Until then, or as an alternative, they can ask an organizer that is present at the event/meeting to stay in the childcare space with them. This person does not necessarily have to engage with the children but must be willing to supervise. We tell volunteers that if neither of these scenarios are possible, we have to decline to provide childcare because it is simply not safe for a KCCA volunteer to take on responsibility for children alone.

Conduct Mantra: We tell our volunteers that at all times when providing childcare with KCCA, we must remain **calm, positive, and non-authoritative**. It is absolutely essential that caretakers not become agitated or angry when volunteering. Yelling, shouting, punishment, and discipline are absolutely off-limits. We are not there to reward and punish children, we are there to hang out with them and provide a safe and friendly environment so that they feel welcome in the space. We encourage techniques like diffusion for when things get rowdy: diffusing a situation like a fight over a toy by calmly and gently introducing a new toy for a child to play with, distracting them with a different game, etc. In the training, we go over a few scenarios that could happen with children and what appropriate reactions might look like.

We created a short list of criteria to help folks know if they qualify for our services and to help us judge as to whether or not we want to take on new partners.

In an effort to remain consistent with our mission and vision, KCCA will only provide childcare services for individuals and organizations who:

• Focus their work on social justice organizing that actively challenges existing systems of oppression
• Challenge the power of the state over people's lives
• Build community-based political, social, and/or economic power
• Would not be able to have childcare otherwise or whose childcare needs are being met by folks who want/need to be more involved in the organizing

Organizations must give us two weeks advance notice when they need childcare. This is in our service user agreement, which we share with any organization or individual that wants to use our services. We require this notice in order to guarantee that childcare will be available at a given event. It is very difficult sometimes to turn down requests because we absolutely want to be there for our communities and we absolutely want their events to be child-friendly. However, one of the main issues we are attempting to battle with KCCA's very existence is the tendency in organizations to treat childcare as an afterthought. There have been several times when organizations have routinely asked for childcare without enough notice and it has provided an opportunity to communicate to them about how that is in and of itself an issue. Without childcare, these events and meetings are inaccessible to a very important group of people (namely women, especially single mothers of color) and their needs must be taken into account from the beginning of the planning process.

Every event requires a bottom-liner. In KCCA, we have it structured so that each organizational partner has a bottom-liner who takes care of coordinating childcare for each of that organization's events. This job entails making sure that volunteers are signed up and present for events, that they have the toys and documents they need, that they are all aware of who they are volunteering with, that there is an appropriate ratio of inexperienced volunteers to experienced volunteers, and that they are in communication with event organizers. We provide trainings that go over all of the online tools we use to help facilitate this process, and our bottom-liners are the only ones given access to our volunteer contact list. We also have a bottom-lining checklist that helps folks remember what all their responsibilities are. Bottom-lining is a serious responsibility. It is also very rewarding work. Importantly, bottom-liners do not always have to be (and often are not) at events for which they are coordinating childcare. They do need to be available to speak on the phone in case something arises, but I personally have remotely coordinated childcare for many events, even when I have been out of the state. In other words, this can be a great role for people who cannot necessarily make it to meetings or rallies but who are good at organizing others and staying on top of the needs of partner organizations.

Our website needs to be kept up to date. The maintenance of our website is crucial, as it is our main resource for curious folks, new volunteers, and interested allies for keeping up with what we're working on. Our front page is dominated by our blog posts, which follow the work of our partners and chronicle the adventures of KCCA. We post our events on our calendar, including when we provide care and when we have KCCA-specific events like trainings, meetings, coloring book–making parties, etc. We keep a public document up to date with our budget including our expenditures, income, and current balance at all times. We have a page ("Docs") with most of the documents we use for organizing available for download. We have a contact form and a PayPal button for donations. There is also a link to our sign-up page so that people can sign up to volunteer through our website. We also have a map set up that shows the locations of our toy boxes and the spots at which we most frequently provide childcare. Keeping a website requires work, but it is an incredibly useful tool that I would recommend for every childcare collective.

Where We Have Ended Up

Kelli's Childcare Collective of Atlanta (KCCA) started out with a long-term vision of being able to provide accessible, quality childcare to a mix of people including a large number of low-income working parents in our communities. Where we have ended up looks a lot different from this original vision. After the first six months or so of organizing free, progressive childcare for radical and progressive organizations in our city, we began researching the ins and outs of becoming registered as a non-profit, what it would take to raise the kinds of funds we would need to open a childcare center, and other such questions. I also read *The Revolution Will Not Be Funded* right around this time. Thanks to this book, our experience with organizing thus far, and many conversations with fellow childcare activists, KCCA decided that we would absolutely not pursue non-profit status.

We decided that when we need money (which hasn't been very often) we can use grassroots fundraising techniques. This has worked very well for us. For one, we make coloring books: volunteers draw pages, we print the images on long paper, we paint our logo on the front with a stencil and we hand-bind the books so that they cost us next to nothing. We sell these radical coloring books with child-friendly images and political messages about issues such as body acceptance, food sustainability, and gender non-conformity at events where we table and at trainings. We have had a fundraising party that brought in a considerable amount and we have had several donors just give us checks when we've needed them. We have never wanted for funds because we don't spend much money and our community is eager to support us when we require it.

We also decided that we would continue to put all of our energy and efforts into making Atlanta's activist spaces more accessible to working mothers rather than allowing our time to be diverted into the enormous bureaucracy that is the non-profit industrial complex. We decided we wanted to remain accountable only to ourselves and to the communities in which we worked, not corporate and rich-people sponsored foundations or rich private donors. We decided that we wanted to create and maintain our own systems of accountability for childcare rather than allowing the state to regulate our structure and our volunteers. We decided we do not want to fall into the trap that so many well-meaning, service-oriented organizations fall into when they become surrogates of the state, performing services that are needed and should be state-provided but are not. Instead we choose to provide childcare for the revolution, for the activists and visionaries and mothers who are doing the work to change the oppressive conditions of society.

Wizards Around the Rainbow
Encian Pastel and the Bay Area Childcare Collective

This comic was developed by the Bay Area Childcare Collective (BACC) and is intended to be used as a tool for anyone doing childcare work. It is based on the participatory workshop, "Transformative Justice and Childcare Work," a collaboration between the BACC and CUAV, Communities United Against Violence on December 15, 2010, in San Francisco. Many of the tips and examples throughout this comic come from the workshop participants.

SO YOU WANT TO BECOME A WIZARD OF TRANSFORMATIVE JUSTICE AND CHILDCARE--

STOP PLEASE! WHAT IS TRANSFORMATIVE JUSTICE, ANYWAY?

I'LL SUMMON THE **WIZE SQUARL** TO EXPLAIN

SQUARL!

POOF!

HELLO.

I SENSE THAT YOU WOULD LIKE TO KNOW ABOUT TRANSFORMATIVE JUSTICE, "TJ" FOR SHORT.

<-Start here

BUT FIRST I MUST WARN YOU-- THIS IS ONLY MY STORY. THERE ARE AS MANY STORIES AS THERE ARE PATHS THROUGH THE SKY.

WHEN I WAS YOUNG, A SQUARL SET OFF ONE DAY TO STEAL ACORNS.

THE FIRST TREE SHE CAME TO WAS THE TREE OF RETRIBUTIVE JUSTICE. IN THIS TREE THE SQUARL WAS IMPRISONED IN A NEST.

SHE ESCAPED.

THE SECOND TREE SHE CAME TO WAS THE TREE OF RESTORATIVE JUSTICE. HERE, THE OTHER SQUARLS MADE HER RETURN THE ACORN AND APOLOGIZE TO THE ENTIRE TREE.

HERE, THE OTHER SQUARLS ASKED, "WHY DO YOU STEAL OUR CORNS?" THE SQUARL REPLIED, "I HAVE NO TREE OF MY OWN AND I AM HUNGRY." AFTER SOME DISCUSSION THE SQUARLS WELCOMED THE THIEF-SQUARL TO SHARE THEIR ACORNS AND LIVE IN THEIR TREE.

SHE CONTINUED ON TO A THIRD TREE: THE TREE OF TRANSFORMATIVE JUSTICE.

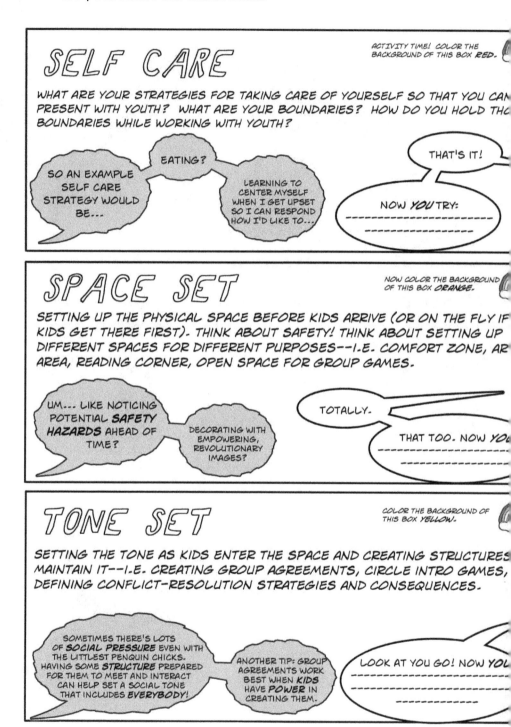

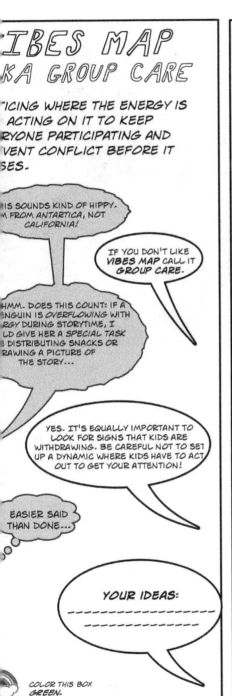

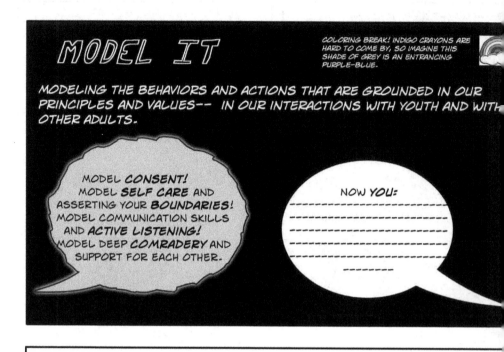

MODEL IT

COLORING BREAK! INDIGO CRAYONS ARE HARD TO COME BY, SO IMAGINE THIS SHADE OF GREY IS AN ENTRANCING PURPLE-BLUE.

MODELING THE BEHAVIORS AND ACTIONS THAT ARE GROUNDED IN OUR PRINCIPLES AND VALUES-- IN OUR INTERACTIONS WITH YOUTH AND WITH OTHER ADULTS.

MODEL **CONSENT!**
MODEL **SELF CARE** AND ASSERTING YOUR **BOUNDARIES!**
MODEL COMMUNICATION SKILLS AND **ACTIVE LISTENING!**
MODEL DEEP **COMRADERY** AND SUPPORT FOR EACH OTHER.

NOW **YOU:**
_____
_____
_____
_____
_____

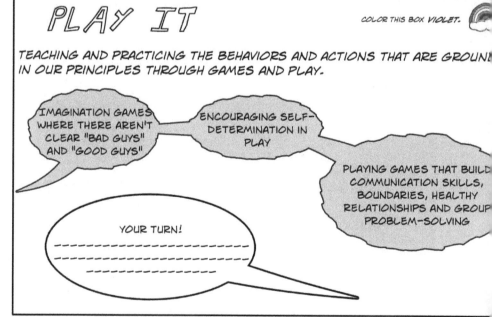

PLAY IT

COLOR THIS BOX **VIOLET.**

TEACHING AND PRACTICING THE BEHAVIORS AND ACTIONS THAT ARE GROUND
IN OUR PRINCIPLES THROUGH GAMES AND PLAY.

IMAGINATION GAMES WHERE THERE AREN'T CLEAR "BAD GUYS" AND "GOOD GUYS"

ENCOURAGING SELF-DETERMINATION IN PLAY

PLAYING GAMES THAT BUILD COMMUNICATION SKILLS, BOUNDARIES, HEALTHY RELATIONSHIPS AND GROUP PROBLEM-SOLVING

YOUR TURN!
_____
_____
_____

PRACTICE TIME

LET'S DO SOME ROLE PLAYS.

OKAY!

THESE SQUARLS WILL HELP BRAINSTORM.

OF COURSE, EVERYTHING DEPENDS ON **CONTEXT** AND YOUR **RELATIONSHIP** WITH THE KID/S. LET'S PRETEND IN THESE EXAMPLES THAT I'M A KID YOU JUST MET AND MIGHT NOT SEE AGAIN. AND...

SOUNDS GOOD.

I'M GONNA SPRAY YOU WITH THIS SPRAYPAINT!

AAAIIIEE! SHIELD THE FACE!

YOUR INSTINCT FOR SELF-PROTECTION IS GREAT, BUT THE SQUARLS RECOMMEND...

–**DE-ESCALATING** THE SITUATION, BY STAY CALM AND CALMLY SAYING "THAT'S NOT COC PUT THAT DOWN PLEASE."

–IF A SIMPLE "NO" DOESN'T WORK, LET THE KNOW THEY HAVE ONE **OPPORTUNITY** TO PU THE SPRAYPAINT DOWN BEFORE YOU **GET TH PARENT OR GUARDIAN.** (IN REAL LIFE THI WHAT WORKED.)

–**CHECKING THE SPACE** EARLIER FOR SAFE HAZARDS SUCH AS ACCESSIBLE BOTTLES OF SPRAYPAINT WOULD HAVE HELPED.

–IF THE KID SPRAYS YOU... STIFLE THE URGE START A PAINT WAR. FOLLOW **YOUR GROUP AGREEMENTS** FOR CONSEQUENCES, INSTE UNLESS IT'S WASHABLE SPRAYPAINT.

I'LL BE THE KID AGAIN.

I'M CLIMBING ON A DANGEROUS LEDGE! IT'S SOOOO FUN. WOHOO

THE SQUARLS SAY...

–**SAFETY IS OUR #1 PRIORITY!** MAYBE YOU WANNA CLIMB ON LEDGE TOO, BUT YOU'RE GOING TO HAVE TO BE A SPOILSPORT SAY "NO." STATE YOUR REASONS FOR SAYING NO.

– GIVE **CHOICES:** I.E. "DO YOU WANT PENGUIN OR PURPLE WIZA HELP YOU DOWN, OR WOULD YOU LIKE TO GET DOWN YOURSELF

–GIVE **ALTERNATIVES:** YOU **CAN'T** CLIMB THERE, BUT YOU CA CLIMB HERE OR PLAY WITH THIS BALL, ETC. KIDS HEAR "NO" AL TIME AND THEY START TO BLOCK IT OUT OR RESPOND WITH ATTIT OFFERING ALTERNATIVES WITH WHAT THEY CAN DO IS WAY MORE POSITIVE.

–TRY **DISTRACTION.** WORKS WELL WITH YOUNGER KIDS.

–IF THE KID ISN'T LISTENING, GIVE THEM A FINAL **OPPORTUNITY** CLIMB DOWN BEFORE YOU **TELL THEIR PARENT OR GUARDIA** (WAIT UNTIL THE KID IS SAFE BEFORE YOU DO. OR HAVE ANOTHER PROVIDER GET THE PARENT/GUARDIAN.)

–AVOID GETTING INTO A POWER STRUGGLE. MAKE IT EASY FOR T TO CHANGE THEIR MIND, NOT HIGH-STAKES.

–TRANSFORM THE SPACE! PUT SOME PLANTS ALONG THAT DANGE LEDGE SO IT'S NOT SUCH AN APPEALING PERCH.

L BE THE > AGAIN.

HEY OTHER KID! YOU'RE UGLY / STUPID / GAY / FAT / RETARDED / ETC!

THIS HAPPENS ALL THE TIME. THE SQUARLS SAY:
—DON'T INTERNALIZE HURTFUL/OPPRESSIVE THINGS THE KIDS SAY. MODEL SELF-ESTEEM. (SELF CARE)

—SET THE TONE: EMPOWERING POSTERS AND IMAGES (FAT PRIDE, GAY PRIDE, POSTERS THAT CELEBRATE DIFFERENCE), GIVE AFFIRMATIONS FREELY AND USE POSITIVE LANGUAGE (IF YOU'RE READING OUT LOUD, TRY SOME CREATIVE MODIFICATIONS! FOR EXAMPLE, I LIKE TO ADD THE WORD "BEAUTIFULLY" IN FRONT OF "FAT" WHEN I READ OUT LOUD.)

—GROUP AGREEMENTS SUCH AS "NO MEAN LANGUAGE" OR "NO MAKING FUN OF DIFFERENCES" OR "NO NAME-CALLING" GIVE YOU A **CONSISTENT MESSAGE** TO **RESPOND** WITH IN THE MOMENT. USE YOUR CONSEQUENCE SYSTEM.

—CONSIDER WHETHER IT'S A GOOD TIME TO TALK ABOUT SYSTEMIC OPPRESSION. IT MIGHT BE, IT MIGHT NOT BE.

—IF YOU'RE COMFORTABLE USING YOURSELF AS AN EXAMPLE, THIS HELPS DIRECT SHAME AWAY FROM THE OTHER KID AND CAN BE A LEARNING EXPERIENCE.

—INCORPORATE BOTH THE CELEBRATION OF HUMAN DIFFERENCES AND ANALYSIS OF OPPRESSION INTO GAMES AND CURRICULUM. ALSO, EMPATHY.

—AVOID LECTURES IN FAVOR OF HELPING KIDS REFLECT ON THEIR OWN EXPERIENCE AND KNOWLEDGE TO UNDERSTAND WHY OPPRESSIVE LANGUAGE AND BULLYING IS NOT OKAY.

—SHAME IS POWERFUL AND IT STICKS. AVOID INCREASING IT FOR EITHER KID IN YOUR RESPONSE.

OKAY, ONE MORE.

I'M GONNA KILL MYSELF WITH THESE SCISSORS!

THE SQUARLS SAY:
—FIRST, ASSESS THE RISK LEVEL OF THE SITUATION. EVEN IF YOU THINK THE THREAT ISN'T SERIOUS AND THE KID'S JUST TRYING TO GET YOUR ATTENTION. ASSESSMENT INCLUDES:

1. IS THE KID SERIOUS? A GOOD WAY TO FIND OUT IS BY ASKING, "ARE YOU SERIOUS?"

—IF IT SEEMS SAFE TO DO SO, TAKE THE SCISSORS AWAY.

—**DON'T** LEAVE THE KID ALONE.

—TELL THE PARENT/GUARDIAN OR A POINT PERSON FROM THE ORGANIZATION YOU'RE WORKING WITH. EVEN IF THE KID WASN'T SERIOUS AND WAS JUST ACTING OUT FOR ATTENTION, THREATENING SELF-HARM COULD BE A CRY FOR HELP. BRING THE INFORMATION TO SOMEONE WHO HAS A RELATIONSHIP WITH THE KID'S FAMILY AND KNOWS MORE ABOUT WHAT'S GOING ON FOR THE KID.

THANKS FOR BRAINSTORMING WITH US!

THESE TIPS ARE INCOMPLETE! YOU MIGHT NOT AGREE WITH SOME! THAT'S OK.

ALSO, DIFFERENT PROVIDERS HAVE DIFFERENT STRENGTHS IN CONFLICT-RESOLUTION. WORK TOGETHER!

LOVE FROM THE SQUARLS. BYE.

I LIKE DOING ROLE PLAYS BECAUSE THEY HELP ME STAY CALM AND CENTERED DURING CRISIS SITUATIONS.

IT WOULD BE SO COOL IF YOU DISCUSSED THEM WITH PARENTS AND OTHER CHILDCARE PROVIDERS.

Activities for Children
Rahula Janowski, China Martens, and Victoria Law

Activities from the San Francisco Anarchist Bookfair:
- Decorate a T-shirt or tote bags. We provided fabric markers and various sizes of thrifted T-shirts and tote bags
- Beads, beads, beads (but don't use in areas with babies/toddlers who could swallow them)
- Playdough (and kitchen utensils to use as toys along with it)
- Big paper on the walls with paints or markers
- Big Legos for the littler kids
- Decorating little flower pots with paints or markers

Recommendations from the Kidz Corner at the Mid-Atlantic Anarchist Bookfair:
- If possible, have different areas for naps, snacks, crafts, and play as well as a comfy chair for a nursing mother
- Offer workshops for kids (such as yoga, storytime, and singing) and workshops by kids! We had an eight-year-old teach button making to all ages, including older people who enjoyed it a lot.
- A Kidz Parade can be a great way for kids and the larger event to interact. In our case, kidz of all ages dressed up and marched around outside and in the bookfair to the cheers of vendors. Our parades tended to be rather surreal and spontaneous. "More Fun" was the first year's theme; "Book Monster" was the second year's. Originally it was a kid's idea, with an adult to facilitate the experience when there are enough kids and adults ready to bust out.
- Provide dress-up clothes, face paints, and a papered a table to sit around and draw on
- Keep the spirit of the larger event. Whatever the parents can get out of it, the kids should be able to enjoy and pick up similar skills. A rad program for rad kids!

Ideas from Kidz City at various events in Baltimore:
- Chalk to draw on the sidewalk
- Jump rope
- Space for youth within the larger room/event: a sofa fort/home made of sheets and blankets, a children's table, a picnic blanket outside
- Activities in the spirit of the larger event; presenters to facilitate activities for youth
- Empty boxes to build houses and rocket ships
- Big soft bouncy ball
- Games like Duck Duck Goose and Red Light, Green Light

The Children's Social Forum at the 2007 US Social Forum in Atlanta had:
- Video-making workshop for older kids. They asked attendees, "Why did you decide to come to the Social Forum?" and edited it into a fifteen-minute video
- A Children's Bill of Rights, to which kids contributed sentences
- Clay-play for making houses and learning about gentrification
- A presentation planned by the nine- to eleven-year-olds and performed to the adults at the closing plenary

The Kids' Track at the 2008 Allied Media Conference in Detroit had:
- Block printing
- A street art workshop about safely cutting and spray-painting stencils
- Political letter writing

Creating Family Space
Jason Gonzales, Revolutionary Parenting Caucus, and a-parenting listserv

Jason Gonzales:

At last year's Anarchist Bookfair in San Francisco, we saw a huge response to the availability of a Family Space where people had a temporary comfortable zone to operate on completely kid-friendly terms with their own kids. In a fun, calm, easy-to-handle environment, a lot of friends of families and passers-by also stopped in to play. The need for an actual drop-off point was quite low, because at most events like this, people are used to having their kids do what they do, and not just because they have to, but because it's healthy and fun. We should work toward making all possible events operate this way, so that there isn't such a thing as a "family space." We all should be able to help out in kid-friendly spaces and be comfortable being around children in workshops and discussion groups, even if some events, such as non-permit protests, may obviously have a higher need for a drop-off point than others.

Considerations from the brainstorming session at the Revolutionary Parenting Caucus at the 2008 Allied Media Conference (AMC):
- At the start of an event, let the audience know that kids and kid noise is both okay and welcome.
- Think about how the conference/event is helping parents/kids/ families get to them. Remember that when flying, bussing, or taking the train, in addition to taking time off work, parents are often paying for more than one seat having to pay for two or more meals instead of one at each mealtime, and so on. How are the organizers working to make the event accessible for lower-income parents/families? Two mothers realized that they couldn't come to the AMC because they just couldn't afford the cost of travel. Both lived in places where it wasn't feasible to get a ride from someone already going or to hop on a group bus.

Ideas from a-parenting listserv:

- Organize non-competitive games for kids to play together; provide art supplies and a space specifically for the kids. We want children of radical parents to become friends with each other and parents to be able to talk to other adults. For actions, have all the kids write "Baby Bloc" or "Kid Bloc" on their signs.
- It is really helpful for organizers to direct parents with strollers to a safe space before a planned arrest situation.
- Tell smokers to point their cigarettes toward themselves rather than at kids' eye level.
- Honor kids somewhere in your readings, if it is at possible to do so. Show kids some positive attention by introducing them, hugging them, playing with them, and giving parents a break now and then.
- Keep toddler-chasers company. If you see a parent doing nothing at an event but chasing a toddler around, it probably means that the parent planned on participating more in the event but cannot. Parenting can be pretty lonely, especially when you're around people you can't talk to.

Don't Forget Familiez on the Rez!
Mari Villaluna

Seven points (one for each direction) on how to support Native American Families
- Understand that entire communities and extended families care for many Native American children. Children are not seen as only a parent's responsibility, but many times a whole tribal community and extended family's responsibility.
- Understand that many times, older siblings have specific responsibilities in taking care of the household and the younger children. This is seen as an honor to support the family.
- Understand that often there may seem to be more than one family living in a house. This is very normal for many families and dates back to many tribes' traditional ways of extended families living together.
- Instead of asking questions about things you may or may not understand, first observe what others are doing, especially if those questions are about spiritual things.
- If a family lives out in a rural area and you live in an urban area, a great way to support is by mailing things that a family requests that may not be found where they live.
- Be respectful of people's bodies and things. Certain things may be used for religious/spiritual reasons. Ask before touching earrings that someone is wearing, or before touching someone's hair.
- Listen to the silence. Be comfortable without talking. Notice how many things are said without even saying a word. Listen to every word children say. They have many stories to tell.

Concrete Ways to Support Parents and Children Fighting White Supremacy from a Pan-Afrikan Perspective

Monalisa Lennon Diallo a.k.a. Oluko Lumumba,
Agnes Johnson, and Mariahadessa Ekere Tallie

Monalisa Lennon Diallo a.k.a. Oluko Lumumba (mother, grandmother, teacher):
The African community needs to connect with its past for strength, knowledge, and spiritual wisdom. If that connection is missing, we will not be able to fight. Building a strong foundation is the key to combating the white supremacist agenda.

- Refuse to give your money to powers that perpetuate a racist agenda.
- Expose our children to as much African culture as possible, past and present.
- Make a vision board with a child.
- Volunteer with your child/children in a community project. It can be picking up trash on the street or identifying the elders in the community and taking their trash out for them.
- Always give children a chance to be around wise elders. An elder dying is like a library burning to the ground.

Agnes Johnson (mother, youth mentor, member of Uthando dollmaker project):[1]
Ragdoll-making as an act of resistance!

- For the Project People Foundation's (PPF's) inaugural project in 1995, 15,000 new black dolls were distributed to black and brown South African children who, because of apartheid, had never seen dolls made in their likeness. This goal was achieved through PPF's mobilization of volunteers in churches, synagogues, schools, colleges, and community organizations throughout the United States.[2]
- Play African music and make dolls with children. The dolls must

---

1. Though she is with the Uthando Project now, she first started a dollmaking project with a friend from Columbia University on a fellowship in South Africa. For more about the Uthando dollmaker project, go to: http://www.uthandoproject.org/about/.

2. http://www.projectpeoplefoundation.org/whoCommitment.php.

be made with black/brown cloth. Use this craft-making as home-made resistance against the deliberate use of "cultural alienation" on our children. Tell stories as you make dolls.

- Teach what apartheid means and about some of the laws that govern it.
- Teach the principal of Kuumba: "Whatever you touch, you will make more beautiful." This is also true for the principles of the Shona artists, the great stone carvers, who say the material already knows what it will look like in the end.
- You can also teach about working cooperatively. Dollmaking projects such as the Black Doll Project are acts of love and giving.
- When the dolls reach children in Africa and a picture is sent back of each child holding a particular doll, a connection is solidified. Parents have written to me years later that the picture is on their mantelpiece. This supports our children in being empowered through the experience of giving to another.
- Remember that Uthando means love.

Mariahadessa Ekere Tallie (mother, teacher, herbalist):
- Don't forget about taking care of yourself first! It's critical.
- A tip for white folks: I went to an incredible talk by Mab Segrest, who wrote *Memoir of a Race Traitor*. Her work and life are dedicated to educating white folks about white supremacy and helping them identify it within themselves and fight it. Mab Segrest is a white woman and one of the things she said that struck me the most was that she knows that she has access to white people in a way that black folk don't. Even though she is saying many of the same things that black folk say, she knows the words can only be accepted and digested coming from her. So if folks want to support black folks in fighting white supremacy, they have to go out and educate white folks.

Holistic First Aid for All Ages
Traci Picard

When taking care of children, whether they are your own or other people's, it is important to have a well-stocked first aid kit for affordably and effectively addressing common illnesses and ailments with both conventional and alternative medicines. Of course, this kit is not meant to replace all types of health care. A clearly posted sign with emergency numbers is a great safety measure in case the assistance of a trained professional is needed. Many minor illnesses and accidents, however, can be safely treated outside the medical institutions.

First, consider the box or bag to keep everything organized. Is the childcare based in a building or outside? Does the kit need to be portable? The size of your kit depends partly on how portable it needs to be, and whether you need access to other resources, such as hot water for tea. You will not want to carry a large cardboard box through the streets, for example, and tinctures, while very portable, can be heavy to lug around. You will need to personalize the kit to meet the needs of yourself or the group. It is beyond the scope of this article to provide all information about dosage or specific uses or safety warnings, but remember to always include instructions in the first aid kit with safety warnings, uses, dosages, and counter-indications.

Keeping a well-stocked first aid kit can potentially cost a lot of money. You may be able to get donations or discounts from farms, herbalists, or health food stores if your cause is compelling. Buying herbs in bulk and making what you need yourself can also be more cost-effective than buying individual preparations. Additionally, many common herbs can be grown on your windowsill and in your garden, cultivated on community plots and farms, or gathered from parks. An endless variety of plants can be mashed up and applied to kids' bumps and bruises, such as comfrey leaf, rose petals, calendula blossoms, pine sap, and the common plantain.

In addition to being aware of potential contamination from lead or toxic waste, pesticides, poop and other types of garbage, however, you should also be mindful to not gather all of a plant from its community, as they need enough to regenerate for the next season. Before harvesting, understand how the plants you wish to gather reproduce and which may be endangered.

What exactly should go into a holistic first aid kit will vary depending on your bioregion, your space and purpose, and the ages and health care needs of the people who need care. Here is a list of some universal basics, and a few extras:

Basics
- Band-Aids
- Children's Benadryl for allergic reactions
- Ipecac syrup and activated charcoal in case of accidental poisoning
- Tissues
- Cotton balls
- Rubber gloves
- Gauze
- Safety pins
- Small scissors for cutting bandages and clothing
- Alcohol-free cleansing wipes
- Medical tape
- Thermometer
- Tweezers
- Rubbing alcohol
- Dried fruit or honey sticks for low blood sugar
- Hydrocortisone or calendula salve for rashes
- Antiseptic cream
- Lavender or rose essential oil spray for calming, and tension headaches
- Propolis tincture for cuts, abrasions, and sore throat relief
- Chamomile tincture for calming and soothing headaches and stomachaches
- Water
- Small plastic bags for icepacks
- Bulb syringe (for suctioning out baby's nose)

Deluxe
- Instant cold compresses
- Catnip, elder flower, echinacea, mint, chamomile, skullcap, lemon

balm, chamomile, fennel, ginger, nettle, oatstraw tea blends to calm stomachs and fevers
- An anti-diarrheal tincture blend of meadowsweet, yarrow, plantain, and marshmallow
- Arnica salve for bumps and bruises
- Aloe and rosewater spray for sunburns, general overheating, and bug bites
- Candied or dried ginger, or ginger syrup/tincture for nausea
- Fennel and dill seed tea or tinctures for indigestion and colic
- St. John's Wort oil or a salve of comfrey, calendula, and St. John's Wort for pain relief from falls, burns or growing pains
- Mullein leaf and elecampane root tincture or tea for a cold with respiratory distress, mild allergies, or asthma
- A bee balm and stage steam for clogged sinuses
- Black elderberry syrup, tea, or tincture for colds
- Apple cider vinegar and honey for sore throats
- Peach bark tincture for allergic reactions, hives, and bug bites
- Anti-fungal black walnut or usnea salve or tincture
- Rescue Remedy for soothing nerves
- Vitamin syrup made of nettles, oatstraw, rose hips, horsetail, and molasses

Further resources:
The Family Herbal by Rosemary Gladstar
Making Plant Medicine by Richo Cech
Peterson Guides, or other identification guides to medicinal plants
Identifying and Harvesting Edible and Medicinal Plants by Wildman Steve Brill
New Holistic Herbal by David Hoffman
Botany in a Day by Thomas J. Elpel

http://www.swsbm.com
http://www.herbwifery.org
http://radherb.org

For involving children:
A Kid's Herb Book by Leslie Tierra
Wildcraft! from http://www.learningherbs.com
Shanleya's Quest by Thomas J. Elpel

I'm a Medicine Woman, Too! by Jesse Wolf Hardin

Sources for seeds and herbs and good information:
Horizon Herbs
Johnny's Selected Seeds
Fedco
Mountain Rose Herbs
Frontier Co-op
http://www.localharvest.org
http://www.farmacyherbs.com

Six
DIFFERENT
APPROACHES

Children
when they ask you
why your mama so funny
say
she is a poet
she don't have no sense
 —Lucille Clifton, "Admonitions"

There is no one-size-fits-all type of support; each family has its own strengths and challenges. Thus, necessary support will look different for each one. In this chapter, parents, caregivers, and allies talk about their distinct challenges—from single parenting among college-age activists to raising children with developmental disabilities, from unschooling to supporting students that most schools have long given up on—and ways that they have worked to overcome them. Support will look different depending on the parents and children involved. The best approach can be to ask: *How can we best support you?*

True empowerment involves supporting parents and children, not assuming that we know what works best for them. Supporting different approaches also means planning accordingly and following through.

Taking Community-Building Seriously
Heather Jackson

My life is structured to fit my daughter's needs and my mothering self. If an event is at 7 p.m., it is hard for me to go. The first reason is that I know there will not be childcare. The second reason is that at 7:30 p.m. my daughter starts settling down to get ready for bed. Thus, my family is unable to participate and our voices are not heard and our presence is not known.

An event at 9 p.m. that provided community childcare could be a child-free night for some families, though it would be too late for my daughter and me. Parents should be asked what time works for them. My daughter is eight years old and has school starting at 8 a.m. Monday through Friday. Any time from 5 p.m. to 7:30 p.m. would work for us, though supper needs to be provided. Weekends are also a good time. If alcohol or drugs are at events, it puts children and their parents at risk; I do not feel comfortable bringing my child to an event where people could possibly be getting drunk or high.

I helped with organizing protests for the Republican National Convention (RNC) and Democratic National Convention (DNC) in Minneapolis. I was helping out with workshops and getting the word out about *consultas* (the large planning meetings). At one of the first *consultas* I attended, I brought up the need for childcare. People were somewhat receptive to it and I was working with a few others on it. There were some issues with safe spaces at some of the actual workshops. The event space had nails and was dirty and was not good for children. We ended up going to a nearby library and were able to provide activities for the children to do. This, however, is an example of childcare not being taken seriously: we had to walk to another space at the last minute. I am sure if the issue had crossed organizers' minds before I brought up that childcare needs to be provided, a new space would have been used. Having to walk a few blocks to a library was an all right option, but we were away from everyone.

One *consulta* that I attended had a safe space house available for childcare. It was refreshing to see that there *was* childcare and the womyn whose house it was had plenty of toys and activities for the children, as well as healthy food choices. I felt comfortable leaving my daughter there. The group facilitating the *consulta* had volunteers for childcare throughout the day and there were other children there. The people involved were taking shifts and drove the children between the house and the *consulta*. However, there were no car seats or booster chairs in the cars, which is another example of childcare and the safety of children not being taken seriously. The organizers could have asked parents to bring their own car seats (if they could) or asked to borrow them for the event.

As a student, I was involved with Students for a Democratic Society. As a mother, I brought up the need for childcare at events. At a talk by Bill Ayers, everyone in the group supported having childcare at events, but at this particular event and others, I was the one who watched my child. No one helped and luckily, my child was the only child there. It was hypocritical for a group to say they supported childcare, but to not help. I was not able to see him speak and afterwards (around 8 or 9 p.m.), everyone went to a restaurant/bar and asked me to go along. Of course, I couldn't, because I had to go home and get my kid to bed. I felt very excluded: not only did I help organize the event, but I had provided childcare, made fliers, and spread the word. Now everyone went to a restaurant, while I went home. I e-mailed Bill Ayers about it as well, though I never heard back from him.

If childcare is happening and only the parents are doing the work, what is the point? Non-parents need to help out so that parents can participate in events. It is also important to look at gender dynamics and see if there are only womyn and trans people doing childcare. Cisgender men can help out too.[1]

Children's interests and activities vary as they grow. This needs to be recognized and addressed in radical communities. Some older kids (like mine) like to help childcare providers with younger kids. Doing so can help them feel included and helps the childcare provider with the younger kids. Different activities need to be provided, too. I am involved with a pro-choice feminist group at the university I attend and I bring my laptop, movies, puzzles, coloring books, crayons, baby toys, and art

---

1. "Cisgender" denotes individuals who have a match between the gender they were assigned at birth, their bodies, and their personal identity.

supplies to our events and meetings. These cover a large array of ages and keep the kids from getting bored.

Some other suggestions:

- Provide workshops prior to events to talk about supporting parents in our communities and providing childcare at events
- Discuss safety and legality issues
- Discuss non-sexist, non-racist, and non-heteronormative childrearing privilege dynamics
- Make sure everyone is comfortable, which includes not excluding people because they are not anarchists or radicals
- Continue to have this conversation!

People need to acknowledge the needs in our communities and realize that most communities have parents and children. If we are going to take our communities seriously, then we need to take this issue seriously.

Equal Access: Community Childcare for Special Needs

Jennifer Silverman

Since I wrote this piece in 2006, the economy has only gotten worse, and services for the most vulnerable populations of our society, like respite care, are first on the chopping block. Most families remain dependent on government/disability funded childcare because we can't afford it otherwise. There is still no cooperative or community organized childcare set up to help kids with special needs in the city where I live. Until our radical communities step up to offer support, those of us who are parents of kids with disabilities will stay dependent on the failing government system, and the time and energy drained by dealing with bureaucratic b.s. and fighting for our needs is time we won't have left to give to any other activism. Supporting your fellow rad parents who happen to be raising kids with special needs would be an important and wonderful first step in the right direction.

I shouldn't be shocked, really. I should be used to it, after all, from the last six years of parenting an eight-year-old with autism. But when I saw this on a public message board of a planned conference for mothers and organized by mothers, I nearly broke my keyboard.

(Identifying information has been changed and the post slightly edited to protect those involved)

> Will childcare be provided at the ___ during workshops or evening events?

> Would the provided childcare be appropriate for a ___ year old with special needs?

> My ___ is autistic and the only way I could go this year is to take ___with me, but I'd also like to participate in the activities.

Reply:

We will have kidshops for ages four to twelve, but we don't have any trained staff who can do special needs . . . all the kidshop volunteers are moms and none of them have children with special needs or experience with special needs.

At the _____ there was a couple who had an autistic child. One stayed with their son while the other went to workshops. Is it possible you could bring another adult with you?

You probably don't understand my frustration. Just to clarify: first, there's the assumption that there is a second adult who can come with this mama and not participate themselves. Second, that this parent can afford to spend the money to bring a second person from halfway across the country to the conference. Third, that the mothers organizing the conference couldn't get their shit together to find someone experienced with special needs kids. Fourth, that without asking what kind of accommodations the parents would need, the organizers simply balked. One kid with autism may need a lot of care while another just may have a slight problem communicating.

This conference was cancelled, so I never got to find out what would have happened.

Imagine that you decided to become a parent. Either all of your prenatal tests came back normal or else you didn't want to do testing, and you figured it would all be fine. You would have this awesome kid who would get to grow up in a progressive community and you'd home-school/unschool, teach gender and racial equality from birth, and wind up with this really interesting, cool, and wise kid who could go with you anywhere. (Granted, this doesn't always hold true for kids without special needs as any activist parent can assure you.)

Then, BOOM!

Your world is turned upside down and you go through the heart-wrenching process of finding out that your kid has a cognitive, physical, or other disability. It gets very, very complicated. Taking your kid to a meeting? Not possible if she's screeching at the top of her lungs or can't sit still. Getting his wheelchair into a non-accessible event space? Not going to happen. So try, on top of dealing with these realities, being physically and circumstantially alienated from the community that you depend on, and not being financially able to pay care providers while being on a wait-list three years long for respite care.

The thing is, in the United States, 17 percent of children have a developmental or behavioral disability including autism, mental retardation, or Attention-Deficit/Hyperactivity Disorder (ADHD), as well as delays in language or other areas (according to the CDC).

But do you see these kids? I used to be really surprised that my son's teachers were shocked to hear how he had gone to the beach or to a museum with me over the weekend. That was, until he got bigger and less manageable and it became much more difficult to bring him out. I firmly believe that my kid—and everybody else's disabled kids—need to be seen, heard, and respected. But at whose expense? If he's not enjoying being there or I'm hopped up on Rescue Remedy, biting the insides of my mouth while trying to keep my shrieking boy from making his otherworldly noises, no one is having a good time.

My seemingly simple solution is accessible childcare and community childcare for kids with special needs. None of the friends we trust with my son had experience with autism before meeting him, but they've really learned how to meet his needs. And luckily he has a fan base of folks who see beyond his disability and love him fiercely. We do have trained respite workers from time to time, but that depends on a lot of factors that are out of our control and it doesn't work out well enough for us to depend on it to continue our work as activists.

I asked some of my mama-friends of kids with special needs to say what they would get from having community-based childcare and what they would want potential care providers to know. Here are their thoughts:

From S: They are really intense and we need help even when we seem like we don't need you there. If you are a care provider at my home so I can do laundry and sit on my ass, then I really do need you still. Even if I just seem lazy.

I am really sorry if my kid hits you, but I didn't tell him to hit you and I don't approve of him hitting you. I'm not going to be shocked or upset for you though. This is the gig.

If you get stuck and need help, go ahead and ask me.

Don't get discouraged if he does things for me that he won't do for you. I promise not to get discouraged the other way.

Please come when you say you're coming. I have all the things I can't do with autism scheduled for your visit, and I really need to do those things, even if they look dumb to you.

You provide sanity for me. I need the sanity pretty badly. You make it possible for me to decompress during my day so I don't freak out and hit my kid or need to institutionalize him to keep from hitting him. You are very very important in my world.

From N: Have patience. Listen to more than words.

Ask parents about what their kids like, what they love to play with, what their obsessions are, how to calm them down. Don't shame the parents for not having toilet trained their child.

About raising our children . . . hmmmm . . . we do the best with what we've got. It is not the end of the world and don't feel sorry for us. There are people out there much worse off than us, and a special needs kid is a kid too. They have feelings that can be crushed by the wrong words.

From me: Instead of assuming you can't accommodate our kids, ask what they need. Then try to meet it. Keep in mind that if you're organizing an event on a college campus or near a university, there are probably students in education or some other field that would love to have hands-on experience with kids with special needs.

Make sure you have backup in case the original person doesn't show. Respect caregiver-to-child ratios. Communicate with parents beforehand. As parents, we are more than willing to provide you with all the information about our kids' needs to ensure they get the right care.

We are still as valuable to our community as we were before we had our kids. Include us.

How Do We Integrate Kids and Adults? What Are Our Expectations about Integrating with Each Other as a Community? (snippets from a discussion on the a-parenting listserv)

Laura Gyre, Simon Knaphus, and
Briana Cavanaugh

Laura Gyre: What I would love to see more than babysitting or anything else, is a discussion or a handout, some kind of statement on community standards relating to children. I realize that could be complicated to get consensus on, depending on process, but it would be cool. The thing that stresses me out the most about taking my baby places is having to worry about whether other people (adults) are willing to deal with their own comfort issues. I am always responsible for my kid's safety and needs, unless someone else agrees to take care of them for a while, but I wish I could let him roam free and explore without having to stop him from touching other people or their stuff. I am fine with other people not wanting to be touched by him, but I wish I could assume that if it wasn't fine, they would deal with it themselves or at least ask me to deal with it without treating me like I had done something wrong. I would like this in all public settings, but at least in radical settings that are not exclusively adult, it would be really nice.

I would also like to know what people's expectations are in regard to noise. I take my little one out of lectures and meetings if he is being so loud that it's really disrupting what is happening, but it's hard not to be concerned if he just shrieks loudly, occasionally. I would like to know whether organizers or people in attendance are concerned about that sort of thing or not.

I had another idea, too . . . providing something like activity packages, snacks or a toy library that people could pick things up from to help support kids who are around different activities with their parents could be cool [at events].

Simon Knaphus: As someone whose kid is not often without a parent, I find great comfort in knowing that when I leave him in a childcare zone, the people there will call me at the drop of a hat. That makes me more free to get involved, not worrying about whether my kid is wanting me. I think that it would be great if, in situations where kids are dropped off, there are a couple of extra cell phones or two-way radios for parents who don't have cell phones as well as a very bold policy about calling parents upon first request or any other expressed need of the child.

I also really like spaces where kids and adults are integrated, rather than just having drop-off, but sometimes that doesn't work or isn't appropriate.

Briana Cavanaugh: I wish adults could handle themselves around kids. I don't mean play with or hang out with my son, but hold their own boundaries, communicate what's going on for them, and let me know. It seems [to be] one of the places where I have to hold other people's boundaries. If I touched someone and it wasn't okay, I'd expect them to speak up and be direct or stop me before it happened: if I were giving a hug, for example. I want people to do that with kids, even if it's more challenging for them—it's their boundary.

Now that my son's ten, he's a pretty good judge of who's going to be okay, but adults behave in unexpected ways, [which can be] confusing and upsetting. Part of that is because we are a very inclusive community, so we get a really wide variety of people.

What's really needed is networks of people we trust banding together, and consistency around that. People willing to step up, for example: it would be great if folks would step up for kid care regularly, so that they can form bonds with the kids and the kids can feel safe with them. That way, we open the circles of trust and support in real, grounded ways.

It would be great if parent-allies who are not parents formed bonds with children to help us hold space at events. For example, there are adults that I know that will step up and work with my son if something happens to/with him when he's out of my sight. I can trust them to help him and speak up if he's been confronted or done something [and they'll] step in if he, say, nearly steps in poison oak.

I'd love to have a term stronger than "ally" for people who don't just care but are willing to step up: allies are people who identify, I want people who are willing to act. Maybe making buttons for them to wear at events so that kids know who to go to if something's up and their Adult on Duty (parents, guardians, or caregivers) are not in immediate eye sight. That would build trust. It would be even more awesome if the kids could give out the buttons so that it was clear that they trusted the adults in question.

What I hear myself asking for is an acknowledged commitment from my peers to support me and my family in ways that I can hear. Reasonable, yes. Do-able? I don't know.

Call to Destiny
A.S. Givens

Tuesday, June 1.

I turn into the parking lot at work just before dawn. I pull the ear buds out of my ears and wrap them around my iPod. I shove the iPod between old bills, receipts, and raw sugar packets on the passenger seat and vow to make my car look less messy. I hang my purse on my left wrist and grab the white plastic grocery bag with nectarines, purple grapes, cherry tomatoes, radishes, a red bell pepper, raw almonds, and sliced Havarti cheese—food that I will eat throughout the day to maintain my physical, mental, and emotional energy. I grab my coffee and my keys, survey my surroundings, and make a mad dash into the building, grocery bag slapping my side, coffee sloshing. Once inside, I pull the door shut, disarm the security system, and breathe.

I work at a school in the Pacific Northwest that serves middle- and high-school-aged students. It isn't the safest of neighborhoods, and we don't work with the safest of kids. Most of the kids are severely emotionally and/or behaviorally disturbed. Some are mentally ill. All of them demonstrate behaviors that don't work for them in a regular school and so they come to this school, the most restrictive environment available, to learn replacement behaviors, coping strategies, and academic skills their home schools were unequipped to teach.

Sometimes the first step for our students is just getting to school. Avoidance, issues at home, refusal to get on the bus, hangovers . . . there are any number of reasons why a student doesn't show up. If we can get them to come to school, however, we can help them work through whatever difficulty they are facing. I am hard on students when they make choices that potentially make their lives more complicated in the future, but life is tough, and these kids are in circumstances that are harder than most. We can support students in meaningful ways, and we do. We have purchased shoes for kids whose feet ripped through the toes seemingly overnight. We've sent food boxes and grocery store gift cards to hungry families. We do our best to fill the gaps, to offer material support and connect families who do the best they can with resources they need. All of that can, and does, happen when the student manages to come to school.

6:30 a.m. My left hand wraps around my *grande* drip coffee (four raw sugars, well-stirred). My right hand clicks the space bar, waiting for my Mac to come to life. I'm a half-hour early for work, but this is normal: I tend to use this time to call students, to plant or harvest my Facebook Farmville crops, or to catch up on the news.

This is my favorite time of morning. The coffee (my third cup, and therefore no longer needed to wake me up) adds to the solitary pleasure of the predawn. It's rich and black and warms my throat and belly.

I have only one student to call today. Drew, our most truant student, enrolled in school with typical emotional and behavioral issues, and a significant concern that his classmates will discover that he's physically a girl. He does his best to avoid coming to school at all. The staff here supports him in many ways that his family doesn't: we call him by his preferred name, use male pronouns, and escort him to the boys' bathroom. Usually it's not enough. For him and some others who have trouble making it to school, I make wake-up calls, and send wake-up texts. Showing up is the first step. If we can get them here, we can teach them what they need to know to be successful in school and in life.

6:45 a.m. When I call Drew, grandma answers and puts me on speakerphone. Not a peep from Drew though I use my sweetest voice. "Get up honey. The bus will be here shortly. We really want you at school today." He won't respond. He tells his grandma he doesn't want to be rude so early in the morning. I wonder what makes the morning any different from the rest of the day, where rudeness rules?

7:20 a.m. Drew's grandma calls. Drew is refusing to get out of bed and she's not going to fight him. I think that's what Drew is hoping for, that his grandma will leave him alone rather than suffer his abuse. I find his manipulation unacceptable and I know she does, too, but she doesn't know what else to do. We fully support Drew as he navigates his gender-identity issues, but he won't make an effort to meet us halfway. He doesn't make it to school that day.

I take special care of Noel, who is having a rough day. I bring him into the office to have breakfast with me. I carry the conversation;

his contributions are monosyllabic grunts and the occasional shrug. I'm worried about him, but I don't push. He'll talk when he's ready. I know he struggles at home: he wants to do what is right, but in his world family is everything and his brothers and cousins are all gang-involved. He feels obligated to run the streets with them and the gang mentality is starting to encroach on his soft heart. He is becoming a bully. I encourage him to take a break if he is starting to feel frustrated in the classroom. When I escort him to class, he squeezes his breakfast orange until it is nothing but pulp.

June 2

Drew's behavior is terrible. I call again, and grandma puts him on speakerphone. I encourage him to get up, get dressed, come to school. I tell him it's half day, that he can make it. Silence. I cajole him to get up. More silence. I tell him that I'm doing my part, that grandma is doing her part, and he has to do his part. He doesn't respond. I tell him to just say "I'm up" and I'll leave him alone. Eventually I hear him tell her to get the **** out of his room. I tell him that's not the most loving thing I've ever heard, but it's nice to hear his voice. I tell him I'll see him in a little bit and grandma takes me off speakerphone. I tell her she can call me back if Drew isn't moving around in a few minutes.

7:17 am. Drew's grandma calls. Drew's refusing to come to school. He's punching walls and telling grandma to get out. I try tough love this time, telling him over the speakerphone that he's not being respectful or responsible. He's not getting an education, and he's not addressing his issues. All I hear is whining. I want to go to his house, pull him out of bed and tell him, "Get to school." He manipulates everyone around him—tells grandma that if she doesn't get out, he will throw a fit. He's always throwing a fit. It must be exhausting.

I get a call from Ms. K. She says her son Will isn't going to come to school because he has a sore throat and she didn't know what to do since the bus was on its way. I ask to talk to Will. I tell him that I am sorry that he has a sore throat, but that he needs to come to school. I tell him that I will give him some tea, bring it to his classroom personally. He says he can't get ready in time, but I know that he has twenty minutes before the bus comes. Oh Lord, I say. I'm a woman and I can get ready in twenty minutes. You're a dude, you can do it. But I won't have time for breakfast, he says. I remind him that he can eat breakfast at school. I'll see you in a little bit, I say. Okay, he says. He's coming. When he checks into his classroom, I bring him a cream-colored Starbucks mug full of steaming Tazo Chai and thank him for coming to school.

June 7

Drew's behavior is outrageous. He's complaining that he's been having nightmares and doesn't sleep. When I tell him that's okay, just get up and come to school, he starts whining and kicking the walls. His grandma is so frustrated she yells that if he can't get it together she's going to put him in a home. She's sick of his behavior. I don't blame her, but I know she's bluffing and I bet Drew does, too. It's time to have a meeting and figure out how we're going to get Drew to school.

June 8

Drew's grandma answers the phone right away. He's up, she said. He didn't want to talk to you or even hear your voice, so he got up. Perfect. I can live with that.

Later in the afternoon I talk to grandma and assure her that Drew isn't the only student with a trauma history. Drew says that he's had a hard life and nobody understands—but he's never given us a chance to show him that we only work with kids who have had miserable lives. We carry them until they have the tools they need to walk on their own. We can't do that over the phone though; Drew has to take the first step by coming to school.

June 9

Drew's not coming to school today. Last night, he took a knife and threatened to cut his own throat. His grandma called 911 and they spent several hours in the hospital. Drew signed a piece of paper saying he wouldn't attempt suicide again. Psychiatric professionals go the contract route when they believe it wasn't a serious attempt.

June 10

Drew comes to school today. We spend some time trying to figure out what he needs to get to school every day. He doesn't have any ideas and isn't willing to engage, so we just sit quietly.

June 11

I call Drew. He's complaining again, but I am able to tell him that he did a really good job yesterday; let's make it another great one today. It is hard to get him to respond and when I do hear him, he tells his grandma that if she doesn't stop shaking him, he is going to piss on her face. Drew, that doesn't work, I say. Remember, I say, if we don't like something that somebody says or does, we can respond in a way that says how we feel without being disrespectful to the ones who care for us. He protests but hopefully he'll make it to school today. I tell him that when he comes, I will be sure to have lunch with him.

June 15

Drew's grandma calls. She wants to be sure that Drew can work in the conference room today. He doesn't want to be around other kids. I assure her that we will do everything we can to be sure Drew is comfortable and able to work, but the expectation is for him to join his classmates.

June 16

I call Drew's grandma again this morning, thinking she is mad because Drew didn't work in the conference room. He came off the bus upset and demanding. Once he was able to get it together, I spent about fifteen to twenty minutes talking to him about his responsibilities and listening to his litany of woes. He went to class and did an awesome job. I am happy to share this with her and she is pleased too. She says he's been in a good mood, knock on wood. I say that I'll do it for her, and she tells me Drew's up and moving around. I'm glad. I hope he makes it to school today.

June 17

Drew's grandma calls. Drew has gotten up by himself. She's happy he's coming to school. I tell her that today's the last day before summer break, but that I will call a couple of times throughout the break to see how he's doing, and then, of course, will start calling when school starts again. Drew needs to have regular attendance.

Drew doesn't make it to summer session. I call him a few times and e-mail him homework, check back and explain the writing and literature assignments. With my baby on my lap, I rest cross-legged on my porch in the fading heat of a summer evening and give Drew permission to text me anytime he wants to discuss the assigned poetry.

Between summer session and the start of the new school year, I call Noel. He's been accepted into a program closer to his home and I'm sorry he won't be back. I'll miss you, I tell him. Make good choices. I want you to be successful. Call me if you need anything. We will always be here to support you, even if you're not our student. Take care of yourself; be good to yourself.

The school year begins on September 8. I call Drew at 6:45 a.m. He is already up and dressed for school. He comes three days in a row. He asks me to text him every morning and I agree. Thursday and Friday, he texts me back right away: *I'm up*. Monday, there's no response to my texts until 9:30 a.m. It's a good that I have unlimited texting, because I text him until he finally answers. *I'm pissed that I didn't come to school*, he texts. *Good*, I tell him. *Come to school. Get an education. You're a rock star, Drew. You're a rock star.*

Supporting Unschooling Families
Sasha Luci

As a pregnant seventeen-year-old, I was scared and already marginalized simply because of my age. My ideals and choices as an eco-feminist, freedom-loving, free-range baby-raising, gender non-conformist, vegan, single parent in NYC further marginalized me. Then I decided to unschool.

Unschooling is the epitome of freedom in and from education. Once you make that choice for yourself, your family and your kids, it is an unending, ever-surprising journey. You never know what will happen next when people are really allowed to be who they are and are fully supported in that process. The concept of unschooling is rather simple: let people do what they want and they will enjoy learning. It's easy.

The difficulties arise with well-meaning friends, families and neighbors who "test" your kids to make sure they are at "grade level" or people who tell your kids they should not be riding their bikes at noon because they should be at school. Or with your own mind panicking when your eight-year-old cannot read or doesn't want to memorize multiplication tables.

Take a deep breath and ask yourself this, when you need to know something that you don't, what do you do?

The answer is you learn it. The method is always different, but you do it, you just do.

It is an incredible gift when children are allowed to learn what they want at their own pace. They can grow into self-aware humans, with intact self-esteem and impeccable critical thinking skills, following from point A to point Z without skipping a beat. Their natural curiosity and love of learning are nurtured for the rest of their life.

That eight-year-old who can't read becomes a ten-year-old who can't stop reading; the kid who doesn't want to memorize multiplication tables becomes an engineering whiz by playing with Legos all day. The things we gravitate towards help us excel in who we want to be and what we want to do. The process is organic.

The hard part is trusting your own organic process over the arbitrary one with which we have been indoctrinated.

People who not only trust that organic process, but celebrate and encourage it are absolutely amazing! Anarchist soccer players have played with our unschool pack; friends at "More Gardens!" have spent time making up songs and spent hours staring at bugs; and traveling buddies have shared responsibilities on the road, making it easy and exciting to go from city to woods to eco-villages. And oh, the eco-villages! They have invited us in to help build straw bale houses and make feasts in the kitchen, all things welcoming to not just me, but my child as well. I have found all these things so much more valuable than any other education choice we could have made.

I have three kids now. It has become interminably more difficult to be my own human, an artist, an activist. My life has become very, very domestic, so much so that I almost forgot who I am until I started writing this. Protest signs have been replaced with mountains of laundry; letters to the senator have been replaced by letters to grandma; zine collections have been replaced by Dr. Seuss collections; the pirate flag . . . well, it's still a pirate flag, but it's on a fort now. My days are full of cooking, cleaning, washing cloth diapers, mediating, and coordinating other people's activities. It's exhausting.

Early on, I would have been judgmental and sometimes downright intolerant of any other choice than the ones I've made. I have grown and changed, settling into a certain level of comfort with myself and my decisions. I have also come to realize that we are all on evolving, complex roads and that the resolutions we come to involve many variables based on who we are and what situation we are in. There is no room left for judgment, just mutual aid. So, yes, I will pick up your kid from school on Friday. I am ready to stop isolating myself and I certainly don't want to isolate anyone else.

I would like my allies to know that when I reach out for help, suggesting that I send my kids to school is not actually helpful. When I have had to be employed in traditional situations, the best support came from people willing to watch my child(ren) *without* recommending I put them in school. Helping them along their chosen path and me along mine, that is helpful. I am so thankful that someone stepped up and volunteered to teach my rockstar to play drums; I am grateful to all the people who still have enough magic left in themselves to go along with my five-year-old

Willow's reality that ze lives in the world of Harry Potter and casts spells and makes potions. By no coincidence, that same child has an amazing memory for plant names and medicinal properties, edible or poisonous. If you go for a walk with Willow, you can be sure to eat borage or some other plant and trust that you are not being poisoned. Thank you, folks, for the walks where you don't mind stopping twenty million times to eat a nasturtium or whatever fruit is in season, or simply to walk on walls.

Thank you to all those who played anarchist soccer with Skyler (now fourteen) and those who take him along to hacker spaces or sit and draw with him for hours; thank you to all you people who take Pacha, just one and a half and so happy to just explore, on adventures with you. You are my saving grace. Thank you to every friend who encourages me to keep writing, painting, organizing. Thank you to all my dear ones who come and have impromptu dance parties in the kitchen: it raises all of our morale.

The thought of schooling crosses my mind every day. I threaten the kids with it when my patience is gone. But what I really need is encouragement to be myself, to hold true to my decisions, so that I (and we all) can help them with theirs. The bottom line here is respect for each other's choices. Respect and freedom go hand in hand in the work towards justice. We have to respect ourselves, our children, our friends, neighbors, allies and even people we don't like that much. So if you want to help, please offer help that fits my values instead of offering advice that just won't work for me. That's ultimately what unschooling is all about, too: the freedom to make choices and be supported in them.

Ways to Support Single Mothers
mama raccoon

I don't have a lot of people around me encouraging my parenting or life choices, or enough people to relieve me from parenting duties when I've run out of energy or patience. Often, I can feel how I push myself physically and mentally to keep going even when I feel that I will fall. Every morning, I wake up and tell myself I'm gonna try again: I'm gonna try to be a good mom, set a good example, make the right choices . . . our lives depend on it! Sometimes, I think: Where is my community? Do people really know what it is to be a single parent? It feels like a lot of responsibility impossible to accomplish, and it's lonely.

I want to know that there are people out there who care! I want to know that we are remembered and understood. I want to know that there are spaces where we are welcome and encouraged to be! I want to know that there are people who want to get to know us and want us in their community.

Ways that community could help:
- The Big Brother/Big Sister organization is one of the mainstream non-profits that does something helpful. We met a really awesome woman who spent time with my kid on a weekly basis. I can imagine a similar program in a radical community.
- Free classes, outings, and events for kids.
- Are you looking for volunteers? Encourage children to volunteer too. Kids like to feel productive!
- Donate food or cook a meal for a parent and child you know.
- Include kid-friendly activities like puppet-shows, sing-alongs, and games at parties
- Organize a sleepover party or field trip for your friend or kids you know.
- Lend a hand. We have plenty of chores!
- As parents, it's easy for us to isolate ourselves. When we're not busy

tending to our needs, we are trying to be all we can be for our kids. Call us up! Invite us out! Remind us that you're there when we need ya, cause we do!

At My Church, We Call It "Radical Hospitality"
Coleen Murphy

When we speak of hospitality we are always addressing issues of inclusion and exclusion. Each of us makes choices about who will and who will not be included in our lives . . . Hospitality has an inescapable moral dimension to it . . . All of our talk about hospitable openness doesn't mean anything as long as some people continue to be tossed aside.
—Father Daniel Homan and Lonni Gollins Pratt, *Radical Hospitality: Benedict's Way of Love*

Radical hospitality is about going above and beyond welcoming; it is about making an environment that is welcoming, active, intentional, and impossible to miss. As someone with children, I have a lot of personal experience of *not* being met with radical hospitality at meetings, of being someone who misses meetings due to some indication of un-welcomeness, and some experience of being actively welcomed. Although the first two scenarios can sometimes make for some juicy venting sessions, I want to tell you instead about what it's been like in the latter, wonderful instances and some of the things that you can do to make me feel welcome.

Name it. Ask "do you need childcare?" Say "children are welcome!" Say it verbally, put it on flyers, make it a normal part of how your organization does things. When I began volunteering with the free clinic in my part of New Orleans just after Katrina, I explained that my time was very limited because of needing to be with my kids, and the community of organizers blew me away with stepping up. Folks would take my kids to the nearby park or to run on the levee or to work in the garden. When organizing meetings and trainings happened, childcare was provided and it was well advertised. Most significantly for me, when I was ready to become involved in the leadership of the clinic and hesitated because of my childcare concerns, one of the organizers told me that as a long-term community member, my input took priority and that recently arrived out-of-state volunteers would support my involvement in ways that my kids and I needed.

Name it again, this time for the people without kids. Let the group know that you are in solidarity with the folks with kids by acknowledging their needs and bringing up the topic so that they don't have to. It gets old to always be the one to do so, to feel like childcare is your own special issue. It's great when an ally is the one to bring up the need and even better when they follow through not just with making childcare/child-welcome happen, but by joyfully acknowledging kids at an event. Marie Romeo, an organizer I've worked with says at the beginning of each meeting how glad she is that the children are present and how delightful it is to hear their voices from the next room, reminding us that they are part of our community. Recently, Gloria Steinem asked for everyone to appreciate a crying baby in the crowd she was addressing. As a parent in the room, hearing a non-parent affirm that kids are a delight and not a nuisance is good and needed. Do it.

Be flexible. Welcome people with kids, welcome people who are kids. Understand that what they need to be present and feel supported may not be exactly what you had in mind. Sometimes, when my children were younger, coming into a space and being told to take the kids to the child-care room felt just as unwelcoming for me as not being acknowledged at all. Some kids and some parents may find it best to stick together at least some of the time, and the group needs to be able to roll with that.

Keep naming it! I just had to say it again because it makes such a difference! Shoot, y'all, I don't even know how to get across how powerful your actions can be. There was a point in the early days of the clinic when several people with whom I'd been working closely were out of town. A meeting was scheduled and the person who called me about it was someone I didn't know well. The meeting was going to be in a new location, apparently a very small space, so I said that might be tough for the kids. The response I got was something like, *Well, I guess they could stay outside on the sidewalk* . . . I said that wasn't going to work for me and I missed that meeting. A few days later, another organizer approached me in a neighborhood coffeeshop and asked if things were okay and offered to fill me in on what was decided at the meeting. When I said I didn't know how I could make it to meetings in the new location, the organizer said, *Hey, your children are always welcome at every meeting. We will figure something out. This is important. How can I help?*

Institutionalize it. This is where I'm at now, the part where we lay things down as policy so that the principles won't get lost. Now that my kids are older, they can usually be counted on to be "good" at meetings by sitting quietly with their books or whatever, so I feel like I need to be extra alert to the needs of my colleague and her toddler as they come to meetings. It's on the rest of us to make sure that they continue to be welcomed to be fully present, and that we celebrate, not merely tolerate, what meetings are like with a ruckus-raising small person present.

Seven

DON'T LEAVE
ANYONE BEHIND

By failing to recognize our interdependence, we jeopardize our ability to sustain each other. For instance, when we buy foods that farm workers have asked us to boycott, we undermine the farm workers' ability to resist exploitation. Although farm workers grow the food we eat, we act as if there were no connection between our circumstances and theirs.
—Mary Wallace, Lee MacKay, and Dorrie Nagler, *Children and Feminism* (Vancouver: Lesbian and Feminist Mothers Political Action Group, 1987).

We recognize *Don't Leave Your Friends Behind* as the start of a longer journey. What about our elders? What about our neighbors? What does access look like to people with language or ability differences? What borders and divisions lie between us? We need to remember that not all families have the same access—for example, while one group of parents may have citizenship, others may not, placing them more at risk not only for detainment and deportation, but the devastation of their families and communities. Even more invisible are those who must leave their own families behind, whose family survival hinges on the most able adults leaving their homes and communities to work hundreds of miles away. In the day-to-day challenges of care work and survival, we need to remember that our fight is not just for inclusion for some, but for justice for all.

Accessibility includes but is not limited to childcare. There are many ways to be excluded. And as several caregivers remind us in this chapter, while we work towards supporting and caring for others, we also must remember to take care of ourselves. We often forget that those who support others also need support.

As we continue our journeys, we connect with more people and learn how our struggles intersect and overlap. We encourage readers to continue exploring ways to build an all-ages revolution that leaves no one behind.

Accessibility
Stacey Milbern

As an event planner and a member of communities that are often excluded, I have learned a lot about what people need to participate.

When have you felt excluded? What do you need to participate? Are there movements or organizations or listservs that you are not involved with because of access or a feeling of being unwelcome?

Accessibility means:

Childcare: Does your event have childcare so parents can participate? Will the kids be safe and have programming so parents don't have to worry about them?

Sliding pay scales: Does your event have different payment options? If people can't afford to pay, can they volunteer their time or services instead?

Different ways of outreach: How do people hear about your events? Does it involve e-mail and Facebook as well as mailings and phone trees?

Gender-neutral bathrooms: Are you aware that trans and gender-queer people are often harassed and in danger when they go into bathrooms? Do you have bathrooms where gender does not matter? Single-room bathrooms are also more accessible for disabled people with their personal attendants or parents with small kids.

Food options: Do you ask about people's allergies or if they need vegetarian, vegan, gluten-free, kosher, or other special food?

Wheelchair and other mobility-related access: How far do people need to walk between events? What physical barriers are there? Are the meeting room doors heavy? Are there chairs? Are they wide enough to fit a variety of people comfortably? It's cool to be creative about making things work, but know that if basic access requires a lot of energy, people may not come.

Structured schedules and awareness of time: How aware are you of time? Do you make a schedule available ahead of time and try your hardest to stick to it? Do you assume that people can stay an hour later if you're behind schedule? How do you communicate schedule changes?

Alternative presentation formats: If people request it, are your documents available in large print, braille, on a cd, or in another language? Did you set aside money for ASL (or other language) interpreters so people can request them? Do people know that they can ask for these things?

Audio description: Is everyone saying names before they speak? If you're giving directions, do you know how to explain it to a person with a visual impairment? If you are watching a movie, does it have audio description or are you prepared to describe what is happening visually? If it is a multi-day event, can you arrange a time where people can go on a tour of the buildings so they know where everything is?

Accessible language: Does everyone know what you are saying? Are you using words that everyone knows? If not, can you explain those terms? Do your documents and presentations have pictures that explain what is happening?

Understanding different learning styles: Are you using a variety of media (documents, videos, audio, pictures) and presentation (large and small group, interactive, hands-on) formats? Are the rooms big enough for people to walk around or stand in during the presentation?

Access to quiet space: If you are hosting an event, do you have a space where people can go if they need to be alone? Do you have flexibility so people can step back if they are getting overstimulated or tired? (For safety at youth events, this works well with a "buddy system" so people can tell someone they are taking a break). It is also helpful to have another lounge where people can go take a mental break and socialize. This also helps clears up congestions in hallways.

Commitment to anti-oppression: Are you committed to creating an environment where people feel safe? How do you handle racist, sexist, heterosexist, ableist, classist comments? How well do you understand the historical context behind what is being said?

Trigger warnings: Do you let people know if you are about to use graphic images, phrases, or stories? Do you consider what is appropriate for children, for survivors of violence, for people with PTSD? People in your audience may be survivors of abuse or have PTSD. Better safe than sorry.

Arrangements for carpools/room sharing: Can you arrange for a message board system so people looking for rides can share?

Identities and experiences: Are you respectful of people's preferred gender pronoun, backgrounds, and disabilities? (Not all disabilities are visible. Go by what folks say instead of assumptions.) Remember that no one ever owes you an explanation for who they are.

Don't Leave Your Mental Health Behind/This Is Not an Endurance Test/My Mamaphesto

Lindsey Campbell

Pills: Want them? Need them? Go on, take a chill pill.

Graphophilia: Always have a pen and paper on hand. Go go graphophilia!

Sleep: Try for six solid hours every twenty-four-hour cycle.

Bedtime: Kids and mama both need a regular bedtime. I savor the moment those lights are out; me time!

Sleepovers: When we host, I get more concentrated alone time because the kid is occupied. When she goes out . . . joy oh joyous joy!

Food: It's good, your body needs it. Open wide.

Floor: Lie down. Go on! Get down there. Get flat. Feel your body and be still.

Breathe: I forget how to do this all the time.

Count: to *ten*. Rinse and repeat.

Lock it: the door. Even for thirty seconds! You can take that power back.

Cinetherapy: Administer a full-length feature film.

Laugh: Just do it!

Frantic? *Stop, drop, breathe*!

Lifelines: Phone a friend. Get on the Internet. Make a connection.

Smile: Find something to smile about, there's got to be something. Work those muscles.

Live: When you think to yourself, "I was supposed to be dead by now," remind yourself you aren't.

Recognize: Saints, angels, beacons of light, pathfinders. Thank You!

Procrastinate: Embrace it like "keeping your friends close and your enemies closer."

Time Out!: "Lindsey, go to your room and don't come out until you've calmed down!"

Sanctuary: A room of one's own, a darkened movie theater, a remote corner of the library.

Read: A book, a magazine, a website, the cereal box, the shampoo label, subtitles.

Hug: Give one. Get one.

Delight: in repetition, habits, schedules, and structure.

Become: the person you want to be.

Be mindful: even when your mind is full.

Hands: I wanna hold your . . .

Love: Say it with feeling.

Music: Make it, listen to it, play it loud.

Hydration: Water, aqua, eau, H_2O. Know it, love it, drink it.

Okay: It's okay to have a bad day, a good day, to be tired, or sad, or even angry. It is certainly okay to be okay.

Yoga: Sometimes this is the only quiet alone time I get. I can't wait for yoga time.

Babysitter: With no family or friends on hand, the number of an eager fourteen-year-old is a must. Fourteen-year-olds think that $20 for the whole night is wicked awesome.

Perfection: is utterly relative and intangible. Let it go.

Write: Blog, journal, type, essay. Get it out.

Confidence: I ain't dead yet, so I must be doing all right.

Trust: I am okay, I will be okay. This is okay.

iPod: Invest in one, keep it charged. Use it and abuse it!

Silence: is not withdrawal.

Parental Caregiving and Loss:
Ideas for Caregivers and Their Allies

Kathleen McIntyre and Cynthia Ann Schemmer

Taking care of people is important work. In our society, women-identified folks in particular may be pressured into taking full responsibility for the physical, emotional, and mental health of others. Some may call these responsibilities reproductive labor or "care work." Despite the fact that all of us, at some point or another, depend on the care work of others around us to survive, it is often undervalued or rendered invisible in our society. For many, taking care of an elder is a full-time job in addition to regular waged employment. The structural oppression that most women-identified folks, people of color, queer, gender variant, and differently-abled folks experience in capitalist society can transform the valued task of parental caregiving into a strenuous burden. Especially with our own parents and guardians, it is often assumed that we will take full responsibility for late life needs, regardless of our other obligations, or our financial and emotional resources. It can be hard to be a parental caregiver without the support of friends, family, and the community. This piece seeks to provide information and ideas for parental caregivers and their allies, both while elder parents are alive and after they die.

Effects of Caregiving

Research has shown that being a caregiver is a form of chronic stress that takes a toll on the body and mind over time and can be very traumatic.[1] Not surprisingly, given our culture's patriarchal norms of female caregiving, daughters and daughters-in-law are more likely to take on caregiving duties for elderly parents than adult male children. Caregivers are more likely to suffer from depression and anxiety and less likely to take care of their own health needs. Because caregivers are likely to suffer from the decreased immune system functioning that usu-

---

1. R. Shultz and L.M. Martire, "Family Caregiving of Persons with Dementia: Prevalence, Health Effects, and Support Strategies," *American Journal of Geriatric Psychiatry* 12 no. 3 (2004): 240–49.

ally accompanies chronic stress, they are more susceptible to physical and psychological illness than those not burdened with regular caregiving responsibilities.[2] It is uniquely difficult to care for parents suffering from dementia because they often become increasingly more agitated, depressed, and confused as their illness progresses. They require more care and often times will not recognize important people in their lives. Caregivers must help parents with complex medication regimens and daily living tasks like bathing, eating, and using the bathroom. They also must help parents navigate confusing and alienating health care systems, and must do so while trying to also balance the demands of their own jobs, families, and lives. Caregiving can take up to twenty hours a week or more and many caregivers end up losing their jobs because of frequent absences.

At the same time, caring for a parent who is ill or dying can be a beautiful act, sometimes mirroring the care we hopefully received from them as children. As radicals, it's important to honor this labor that defines our humanity, and support those who are engaged in it. Recognize that those caring for ill or dying parents might have many odds against them. Share the load if you can: cook a meal, watch the kids, come over and clean something, offer a ride, walk the dog, or take them out for small pockets of relaxing time. Also, understand if they have to leave early or suddenly, want to stay sober, or need more emotional support than usual. Research has shown that caregivers who have regular time to attend to their own needs are less likely to become burnt out. Community members and friends can help with this.

Anticipatory Grief

When parents are ill or suffering for a long time, we begin to prepare for their impending or possible death by imagining what life will be like without them. This is a way for our brains to begin the long task of trying to make sense of a profound loss before the loss has actually occurred. This process is sometimes called "redefining," and means different things to the different people affected by the illness. For example, the role of "daughter," "son," or "child" can take a very different form during caregiving; parent and child roles might be reversed, confused, or simply changed as we scramble to adapt. Anticipatory grief does not mean that one does not also grieve after their parent dies, but can help us to understand the pain, anxiety, and search for meaning that often accompanies long illness with uncertain outcomes.

---

2. Ibid.

Parental Caregiver Self-Care Tips

Make time to go to regular doctor's appointments and checkups *for yourself* if you can afford it. Try to allot time for physical activity or just time for yourself (a brisk twenty-minute walk, a weekly movie night, basic stretching and deep breathing, a bath). Go to weekly counseling, attend a caregivers' support group, or start a caregivers' support group in your town. Some caregiver networks and listservs can be found online if your mobility is limited because of caregiving responsibilities.

Supporting a Caregiver

As a friend of a caregiver, you have the unique ability to remind them of themselves, what they enjoy, and who they are. Care taking cannot occur at the expense or loss on one's self, or everyone will get burnt out. Gentle yet consistent reminders to your friend that you love and value them are important. Get the community involved—make a Google spreadsheet that everyone can contribute time and tasks to. Send out an e-mail "Wish List" for time and resources that would help lighten the burden. Benefit shows, readings or workshops can be held to raise funds for a caregiver or elder community member.

Parental Loss

Parental loss stirs up fears in all of us. Everyone's parents are going to die, but we live in a culture that rarely acknowledges this reality. We usually have great difficulty finding the words to say to someone who has lost a parent, both because we rarely learn how to speak authentically about loss, and also because the words we might say are so easily drowned out by the crashing sounds of our own reactions in our heads. The first thing for you to do when supporting someone throughout this is check in with yourself about your fears, experiences, feelings, and barriers so you can be present with them. Acknowledging these things helps you to be in touch with them instead of pushing them away. If you are in touch with these fears, you may even be able to use them to help support the person by allowing yourself to empathize with how they might be feeling.

There is no statement or action that can take away the pain of grief, so think of your support in terms of "bearing witness" and "being present with." Active listening, without giving prescriptions for action or thoughts is most helpful. Instead, help a person to share with you what's going on for them in that moment.

Instead Of: Try Saying

They're in a better place/at least they are no longer in pain:
How do you think of your parent now that they are gone? Do you believe in an afterlife? Do you still feel a connection to your parent?

You are so strong/I'm so sorry:
Is there anything I can do to help you cope?

This was God's plan:
What are your spiritual or religious beliefs around death?

Death is just another part of life:
Aside from their physical presence, what else do you feel you have lost? Is there anything I can do to help with these absences?

They will always be with you:
How can I help you to keep their memory alive?

Everything happens for a reason:
How has this experience affected your sense of safety, routine, and expectations about how your own life would go?

Time heals all wounds:
How are you feeling right now? What can I do to help you in the long run?

Just remember the good times:
What do you remember most about your parent? Do songs, foods, places, or objects remind you of them? How does that feel for you?

Don't cry/calm down:
This one is best replaced with simple willingness to sit with someone while they cry/yell/emote.

Note that most of the things to avoid are statements and most of the things to try are open-ended questions. Get the person talking! It will help them to make sense of things bit by bit. It also gives them space to talk about and remember the deceased if they wish to do so. Those who are grieving often avoid this out of fear of making others uncomfortable or they may believe that no one cares. These questions will show them that you are interested in their feelings and their relationship with the deceased.

Notably, if you are supporting someone who is grieving the loss of a parent, you have now become a caregiver and it's important that you continue to take care of yourself. If you are having trouble being there for the person, say so. It will better that they hear it rather than think you've stopped caring when you begin taking time for yourself. Talk it out. Don't be afraid to set some boundaries for yourself. Sometimes grief can feel so overwhelming that the person going through it is not even aware of how hard they might be leaning on you. Help them to seek out and connect to resources like zines, books, music, mental health resources, and community events that might comfort them. Grieving people are likely to have trouble concentrating on everyday tasks and logistical planning, so give them phone numbers, contacts, and information if they are interested in trying something out.

No age to lose a parent feels acceptable, even if the parent died at what our society considers to be a "natural time" in their life. There is always potential for a very specific and strong experience when someone loses a parent. Older adults are often met with a dismissive attitude towards their grief, as if, since it happened "at the right time" they should not need to process it. Conversely, younger people who lose parents often have few peers with similar experiences and the isolation can be profound. Additionally, our relationships with our parents are often very complicated. Perhaps they had mental health issues, addiction, were abusive, or were absent. Complicated grief exists and is okay. It's fine to feel anger, hatred, relief, and happiness when a parent dies, no matter what society tells us.

Thinking about Grief in General

In a society that tends to seek containment and denial of human suffering, rational and linear models of grief, such as Kübler-Ross's stage model are widely accepted as "norms" of grief expression. In this stage model, we are expected to move through denial, anger, bargaining, and depression, and from there into acceptance, indicating a healthy adjustment to loss.[3] However, those who recognize the massive variation across grief experiences often prefer a "spiral" model, in which

---

3. Elisabeth Kübler-Ross, *On Death and Dying* (New York: Scribner, 1969).

the feelings listed in the stage model can be repeated or revisited over time.[4] A third model proposes the following three non-linear "tasks" of grief and healing: accepting the reality of the loss, experiencing the pain of grief, and adjusting to life without the deceased.[5] These tasks can happen simultaneously and unevenly over time, leaving room for a spectrum of different emotions and responses to grief. Currently, mainstream psychology recognizes "bereavement" as a period of adjustment after someone dies that lasts for two months, and any grief reaction lasting longer than that must be automatically classified as "major depressive disorder."[6] A radical revision of this classification system would assert that grief is not a disorder, but a necessary and natural response to the loss of an important person in our lives. Reclaiming our need to work through our grief processes in our own way and at our own pace is a way to reassert our humanity and the importance of human connections within the dehumanizing capitalist system.

Especially with unexpected or sudden losses, we may experience a roller coaster of positive, neutral, and negative emotions lasting a few seconds to a few hours and then changing to something else. It may feel confusing to keep up with these changing feelings, which are evidence of the brain's attempts to literally make sense of the fact that someone is not here anymore. Our brains are naturally programmed to resolve the impossible truth of death over time, just as children are naturally programmed to form complex attachments to caregivers. Trust the process, whether it comes in stages, spirals, or tasks, and know that time is working. If you are feeling stuck, explore counseling options: many Hospice Care centers offer bereavement groups, or you can explore group and individual therapy options here: http://therapists.psychologytoday. com/rms/.

Further Resources
Books
Patrimony: A True Story by Philip Roth

---

4. Sameet Kumar, *Grieving Mindfully: A Compassionate and Spiritual Guide to Coping with Loss* (Oakland, CA: New Harbinger, 2005).

5. J. William Worden, *Grief Counseling and Grief Therapy: A Handbook for the Mental Health Practitioner* (New York: Springer, 1982).

6. K. Shear and H. Shair, "Attachment, Loss, and Complicated Grief," *Developmental Psychobiology* 47, (2005): 253–67.

Final Payments by Mary Gordon

Motherless Daughters: A Legacy of Loss by Hope Edelman

Caliban and the Witch: Women, the Body, and Primitive Accumulation by Silvia Federici

The Mercy Papers: A Memoir of Three Weeks by Robin Romm

Living with Grief When Illness is Prolonged by Kenneth J. Doka and Joyce Davidson

The Work of Love: Unpaid Housework, Poverty, and Sexual Violence at the Dawn of the 21st Century by Giovanna Franca Dalla Costa

Waterbugs and Dragonflies: Explaining Death to Young Children by Doris Stickney

Websites

Family Caregiver Alliance: www.caregiver.org (click on the "groups" tab; they also have a group especially for LGBTQ caregivers)

Today's Caregiver: http://www.caregiver.com/ (has lots of information on caring for people with different types of physical and mental illness, caregiver support tips, and a "Local Resources" section to help you find groups in your area)

ElderCare Online: http://www.ec-online.net/community/Activists/can.htm has a place where you can chat online in real time with other caregivers, as well as a list of Caregiver activists and mentors.

Concrete Tips for Caring for People with Alzheimer's and Dementia: http://alzonline.phhp.ufl.edu/en/topics/#T_CareWell

Un Corazón separado por una frontera/A Heart Separated by a Border

Ingrid DeLeon (translated by Carina Lomeli/POOR Magazine)

As you read this beautiful piece by Ingrid Deleon, please understand that as a colonized and oppressed people in poverty, we do not speak the colonizers' languages with academic precision. We resist linguistic domination by writing and speaking and creating. There will be typos and different uses of language. These are our voices, our art, and our resistance narratives. Read them with love and spirit in your hearts. Decolonize your mind one page at a time.

For English read below

El hielo se empesaba adesconjelar. Por los fuertes rayos del sol una mañana. Como a las 7:30 am mi hija me abrazo me dio un beso y se despidio. Mis baronsitos me veian como diciendo? Que pasa, porque mi mama se va y nos deja?

Abraze a mi primer baron con el alma pues el solo tenia 5 años. Le dije pase lo que pase no olvides que te amo. El agacho la cabezita y me dijo esta bien. No llore pero sentia que la respirasion se me aseleraba el triple de lo normal sentia que mi cuerpo se estaba quedando sin su corazon luego abraze ami bebe y sentia que nuevamente lo perdia. Lo abraze mas fuerte lo bese con los labios temblorosos porque queria llorar. Le dije ya me voy hijito no vallas a llorar, no se cuando voy a regresar pero te amo. El solo dijo bueno mami se sonrrio y me dijo pero seapura mami me trae una paleta y un pan. El tenia solo 3 años y pensaba que yo hiba regresar pronto y asi siguio gritando hasta que ya no me vio en ese momento yo llore porque ellos ya no me veian. En todo el viaje lloraba pero traia una meta y tenia que cumplirla y no queria regresar pues no me gusta ser cobarde.

Son 7 años que no los veo de amargura de llanto por no tenerlos conmigo no verlos creser.

No saber cuales son sus gustos cuales son sus pensamientos cuales son sus alegrias, cuales son sus corajes Pero de algo estoy segura es que mi amor crece mas cada dia. Ellos lo saben, es que los amo y ellos a mi, talves la distansia nos a hecho valorar el amor verdadero que nada ni nadie lo hara romper.

Mi corazon ya los quiere verlos abrazarlos besarlos sin parar, que no exista el reloj ni el tiempo para separarnos aunque la sonrisa inocente de mis hijitos lo conservo en el fondo de mi corazon haora que mis hijos hablan conmigo, me siento emosionada ellos dicen mami la amamos y la queremos muchisisimo la extrañamos y queremos que se venga, queremos verla pronto y esas palabras me llenan de satifaccion.

Asi como mis hijos estan creciendo sin mi, hay muchos, mas esta situacion.

Y siguen quedandose sin sus padres por la pobreza por que el gobierno en nuestras paises no hacen nada para cambiar la situasion y por eso esque mis hijos y a otros niños estan como dice María Helena Jiménez, procuradora 15 judicial de familia de Caldas, se refiere al fenómeno denominado 'huérfanos con padres vivos'.

Yo entiendo esto porque mi mama siempre dice lo mismo que mis hijos estan huerfanos porque a pesar que tienen a su padre cerca y mi con vida. Si yo no estuviera? que seria de estos niños dice ella.

Hay una estimacion, 2009 50 mil niños están creciendo sin sus padres, quienes migraron a otros países

• • •

The rays of the early morning sun started to melt the ice. It was 7:30 am. My daughter hugged and kissed me on the check and said farewell. My little boys looked at me as if asking themselves, What happened? Why is our mommy leaving us?

I hugged my first son with all my soul. He was only five years old. I told him, "No matter what happens remember that I love you." He lowered his head and told me, "Okay." I did not cry but I felt that I started to breathe three times faster than normally, I felt my body losing my heart, I hugged my baby, and I knew I was losing him again. I gave him a big hug and kiss, my lips shaking because I wanted to cry. I told him, "Now I must go. Please do not cry. I don't know when I'm coming back, but I love you." He only said, "Okay mom," and smiled and added, "Okay, but hurry up mommy and bring me a popsicle and some bread."

He kept saying this until I disappeared, and at that moment I began to cry because I knew I wouldn't see them soon. I cried through my whole journey, but I had a goal and I needed to reach it and get to the North, and I wouldn't come back because I don't like to be a coward.

It has been seven years that I have not seen them, and I feel bitterness and sadness for not having my kids and seeing them grow.

It has been seven years of not knowing what their tastes are, what their thoughts are, what makes them happy, how they get angry. But there is one thing that I am sure of, and that is they know I love them and they love me. And maybe the distance has made us appreciate true love that nothing or nobody can break.

My heart wants to see them and hug and kiss them in person. I want to see them now and hold them without stopping, kiss them without end. I wish that time did not exist and would separate us apart. I remember the smiles and keep the memories in my heart. Now and then when I speak with them by phone, I feel happy to hear their voice they say that they loved me, that they miss me a lot. They say they want to see me soon, and hearing this fills me with satisfaction.

Just like my children are growing up without me, there are many more in the same situation.

Many children live without their parents because of poverty, and the governments of our countries don't do anything to change the situation. This is why my children and other children are in this situation, according to María Helena Jiménez, judicial attorney for the family of Caldas. She refers to the phenomenon of "orphans with living parents."

I understand because my mother said the same thing about me. She always said my children are orphans despite having a father close by to them, and me alive. If I was not here what would be the future of those children, she would ask.

In 2009, fifty thousand children are growing up without parents, who have migrated to other countries.

Through All The Transitions: A Duet on Caregiving, Family, and Community

Jessica Mills and Amanda Rich

It's going to be a long night. Vovo is up sick again and April and I are both tending to her. We are taking turns, but because we both care about her and are trying to diagnose how bad her malady is, even our resting moments are tinged with worry. If you are a parent, or have ever cared for a sick loved one, you know how these moments are the mortar that build our families by making us more resilient. The capacity of our hearts increase as they strain to open just a little wider as we enact compassion. Stepping out of our egos as caretakers we attain a glimpse of nirvana.

My partner Ernesto and I jokingly lament that we've been tired for over eleven years now. There's our paycheck work, community-building work, and work on our additional life-fulfilling projects, but on top of it all, the work that takes priority is being caregivers for our two school-aged daughters. It's exhausting work, attempting to find balance for everyone's physical, emotional, and other needs to be met. But we are a team, a family, a commitment. And because our parenting style is guided by our anarchist ideals, and love, we put in some long hours that leave us wiped but thankful that our efforts are helping to create at least some of change we wish to see in the world.

Or at least that's what I tell myself when it's two in the morning and I'm on my hands and knees cleaning copious amounts of caca off the bathroom floor. Nirvana. Compassion. I would only do this for someone I truly love. Our child? No. This person bears no blood relation to me. But her life is forever layered in brick with mine now. This person is my partner's grandmother, Delfina, but we call her Vovo.

But that thankfulness comes with daily challenges, and it's hard to remember that love-filled satisfied feeling when attempting to negotiate the third sibling feud of the day and my ideal parenting practices take a back seat to my falling back on a more fight-or-flight stress response. Deep breath. Love. Patience. Respect. Remember that we are individuals intertwined as parts of each other. A family of individuals who need others in our lives who share the desire for building healthy relationships as a foundation for that change in the world we wish to see.

Unlike the birth of a baby and the joy of watching that life unfold, we are sitting with death and the unraveling of a brilliant spirit and a strong woman whom we both admire. As friends and allies of parents we have been a part of "new family support": bringing meals, sending cards, offering to help clean or provide childcare. Now, on another curve of the same cycle, we find it difficult to elicit more than a "wow, that must be so hard," kind of comment from our friends. Maybe it is because, as women in our thirties, it is rare that our peers have experience as caretakers for the elderly. Also, we are grieving the loss of a person whom we love and perhaps there are few who want to sign up to share that grief. Either way, we often feel "left behind."

When the girls were babies, toddlers, then preschool-aged, the support we needed from others in our lives was different from what our needs are now. Though our circle of friends did shift significantly when we first became parents, folks in our community were generally supportive in material and concrete ways. We'd lived among that community for many years and have since moved three times. As a result, we've learned important lessons in the necessity and hard work of community-building. Each move prompted a new search for mutually supportive community; it also prompted a re-evaluation of what our family needs were and a reevaluation of what the girls' needs were as their needs change with their development. During that process, it's hard not to feel isolated and disconnected because of the patience required. It takes a good amount of time to "move" into a new community; it was not realistic of me to just pop onto a new scene and expect immediate mutual support.

Recently, my partner and I both attended (on separate days) a city-sponsored group counseling event for anyone who is "a caregiver." One thing that struck me was the shared sense of isolation. Unlike taking your child to a park or playgroup where you might find like-minded parents with whom to swap childcare, many of our loved ones are homebound, keeping us homebound. Rarely do we come across anyone who shares a similar story. Sometimes I scan the grocery store and see a woman shopping with an elderly man and wonder, "Is that her father? Does she live with him?" Or I see a woman who looks on the edge of sanity for lack of sleep, her tired lines matching mine. I want to ask, "Is someone you love sick? Let's go have coffee and cry together." As if we would have time.

I've got time to dream up an amazing, sustainable, committed mutual aid–based community support network, but not the time to organize and mobilize. My dreaming is interrupted by my needing to help prepare some food, open a locked door, and remind my big girl that the chickens need to be cooped when the dogs are out. So my heroes are those childless folks in our community who turn themselves into allies by organizing free after school dance and art classes. They are the fellow dreamers who organized Farm Camp, a day camp where we working parents could take our kids when school's out for summer. They are the older schoolteachers who have the summer off and whose own children are grown, so they round up neighborhood kids whose parents are working and take them to the public pool, community garden, and library. They are the radical women who recognize that my on-the-verge-of-adolescence daughter needs them as she naturally pushes away from me, her mother. They include her in their gaggle of other preteen girls and help them foster healthy friendships with each other, mentoring and modeling.

In addition to dealing with our grief, we also have to deal with our family. Many radical folks I know are not close to their immediate family. Indeed, my partner and I both live about 1,000 miles away from our parents. In raising children, we look to our communities, the families we have built together. However, with Vovo, we have to be in constant communication with April's family. We are lucky to be more or less on the same page. But when we disagree we cannot hang up and refuse to negotiate differences or hurt feelings. We have to muddle forward, making arrangements, discussing money, updating them on what the hospice nurse has said.

Living thousands of miles away from immediate family, our community saves our sanity and helps us combat nuclear family isolation. We purposefully get involved with community organizations that welcome and involve kids in their work. It's mutually beneficial that way; everyone wins. I take time to dream up even more ways that a mutual aid–based community support network could grow. Beyond organizations welcoming and involving kids in their work, what about having part of their work taking on kids as interns and apprentices? Where are the youth centers in every town and city? Where are the well-greased mutual aid societies to co-house with?

The decision process for bringing Vovo into our home was similar to conversations we had about adoption or trying to conceive a child.

In some ways our lives mirrored our heterosexual friends. We bought a house (with extra rooms), we made a commitment to each other. Our lives have changed completely and in ways we could have never anticipated. And of course there is the divine poop. And for every moment of scrubbing shit, there is a moment of song. With a smile and mischievous look she changes the words to the Portuguese folk songs we are belting out on the front porch. Adding some snippet of the present moment to a song a hundred years old. The new release has a phrase like "Nanda made nice lunch" or "Whaddaya want me to do?" And just like children, she teaches us. Vovo says everything is "half and half; not too good not too good; not too bad not too bad." She will never say she is okay—although she doesn't have a problem complaining. But, in the roller coaster of her ups and downs, we find a rhythm and a ride we are not entirely opposed to being on.

Before kids, I knew the importance of community, but not until I had kids did I really feel it. In this sense, they have been my teachers. Ernesto and I became parents on purpose but without any real planning. I had planned on being the primary caretaker while Ernesto was a full-time student, but had no idea I was in for feeling cut off from my pre-kid life. I learned just how important community is while learning how to take care of a baby, how to parent in a way that reflected our ideals, how to met my own needs at the same time, and how to get anything else done. All of that is just too much for any one person to do. It's a recipe for nuclear meltdown.

Just like two new moms, we are trying to find balance. Between the push and pull of giving and taking; working and resting; scrubbing and singing. Like many new families we are establishing a schedule that works for us, that fits our personality patterns and necessities of down time and work. And sometimes we schedule dates. Occasionally we found a friend or two, mostly with small children, that would come and sit for a few hours with her. Eventually we hired a service that was outrageously expensive—imagine paying $20 an hour or more for a baby sitter! But time outside the house together was essential, not only to keep our relationship intact, but also to give ourselves the break we needed to continue to be the best caregivers possible.

Home life is lived with constant interruption and constant checking and balancing genuine needs against temporal desires. I know I cannot accomplish certain tasks while kids are awake, so I have become more skilled not only at time management and prioritizing but also much better at communicating what my own needs are as well as negotiating about who's going to be able to get what need met when. Things that require less concentration, like making flyers or organizing via e-mail, or things I can do with kids, like distributing the CSA out of our front living room, are accomplished during their wakeful hours. After they get to sleep for the night is when I can concentrate without interruption, so that's when I write, grade papers, plan lessons for the classes I teach at the community college. But wait, where's the partner time? Oh, there it is, made possible by deliberate mutual aid–based community-building efforts in the form of date night childcare swapping with neighbors. Sounds terribly unromantic due to the lack of spontaneity, I know, but we've learned that without it, we get unhappy due to the disconnect with each other and are just too tired to spend quality time with each other if we only wait until the girls are asleep for the night.

Of course there have been friends with whom we have lost contact because our ability to give and go out has shrunk significantly. At least in the way that best suits them. Most have been flexible, forgiving our absences and absent-mindedness. Especially when it comes to social graces. We used to throw a lot of parties. Now it is hard to remember my own birthday and come up with some gumption to celebrate it, let alone the birthday of anyone else. But getting back to the feces and the folk songs. Families need support through all the transitions: New baby. New Vovo. Adoption. Separation. The formation of new family units. Moving. Changing. Growth. There are larger lessons of building trust and community. There are stories of too much worry and not enough sleep. There is joy beyond any earthly description. I cannot possibly write all the scenarios here. But the song is the same.

The physical dwelling we live in represents a single nuclear family house. But with the community we live among, we transcend our nuclear family housing arrangement. We live beyond our walls in a way that's more than building an extension off of a utility room. Our community has become a foundation on which to build. Like our girls keep growing and changing, so do our needs morph with those of our community. Keep framing, keep laying brick, keep patching the roof. Keep organizing, keep living, keep loving.

Contributor Biographies

The Bay Area Childcare Collective offers childcare resources to grassroots organizations composed of and led by m/others who face multiple oppressions, primarily by providing competent and politicized childcare to low/no income immigrant m/others and m/others of color. For more info: www.bayareachildcarecollective.org.

Ramsey Beyer is a full-time nanny and comic artist living in Philadelphia, PA. She's currently working on her first comic book, *Year One*.

Rozalinda Borcilă is interested in how relations of power and domination are produced, experienced, and contested in daily life. She is an artist, educator, writer, and mother and is active in self-organized collectives such as Compass Group, Mess Hall, and 6Plus.

Mariah Boone is a mother, writer, social worker, and teacher living and writing in Corpus Christi, Texas. In her spare time, she is the publisher of the online zine *Lone Star Ma: The Magazine of Progressive Texas Parenting and Children's Issues*, the leader of two Girl Scout troops, a First Day School teacher, and a union thug.

Marianne Bullock has been a practicing doula for over seven years and currently serves as a Lead Doula with the Prison Birth Project, providing full spectrum doula care for women in her community in Western Massachusetts. She is pursuing a degree in Social Justice & Environmental Studies at a local community college and has led workshops on addressing sexual assault in activist communities, empowering birth, and prisons as agents of reproductive oppression. She is the mama of the wildest three year old.

Lindsey Campbell is a full-time grad student, single-mom, projectionist, and writer living in Montreal, Quebec, Canada. She hosts a bi-weekly podcast "This Manic Mama" on hipmama.com radio, and a monthly radio program "In the Motherhood" with Trixie Dumont, on 90.3 FM in Montreal. Her writing has been featured in *HipMama*, *Mothering* Edmonton's *Vue Weekly*, and *Birth Issues Quarterly*.

Briana Cavanaugh has been a community organizer for more than twenty years. Her focus has been primarily on collaborative "human services" public policy with a love of community and spiritual group facilitation. She's been an activist single mom since 2002 and made the surprisingly terrifying leap to homeschooling her tween in 2010, by his request.

CRAP! Collective (Child Rearing Against Patriarchy) is a network of parents, educators, and allies who want a feminist upbringing for the next generation. Based in England, they support and discuss feminist childrearing issues and push childrearing issues in feminist activist circles.

a de la maza pérez tamayo is a fabulously Deaf, queer migrant person of color living and resisting in Arizona. Ze currently spends most of hir time plotting ways to non-violently dismantle white supremacist capitalist heteropatriarchy and sharpening hir unapologetically anti-racist, anti-(cis)sexist, anti-ableist, anti-classist, sex-positive, nerd-positive, pro-migrant, anti-capitalist, queertastic community-building parenting skills.

Ingrid DeLeon is a poet, clothing designer, actress, *Prensa POBRE* reportera, mama of four children, poverty and im/migrant scholar in residence at POOR Magazine, and author *of El Viaje: The Journey of One Immigrant Mother*, published by POOR Press.

Clayton Dewey is a radical papa to three beautiful and inspiring children. He works as a web developer promoting the open source movement and is a co-editor of the online magazine *The Precarious*.

David Gilbert was a founding member of Columbia University Students for a Democratic Society and member of the Weather Underground Organization. After eleven years underground, he was arrested with members of the Black Liberation Army and other radicals following a botched armored car robbery in 1981 and sentenced to seventy-five years in prison. Before going underground, he provided extensive childcare via his Men Against Sexism group in Denver. He is the author of *Love and Struggle: My Life in SDS, the Weather Underground, and Beyond.*

A.S. Givens is a blogger and non-fiction writer, with work published in the 2009 anthology *My Baby Rides the Short Bus* and on www.momlogic. com, www.trusera.com, and www.seattlepi.com. She has been married for seventeen years to the love of her life, Charles Givens, who gives their family unwavering support, strength, and commitment. She is a determined mother to Maya, Zion, and Elijah Givens. She lives and works in the rainy Pacific Northwest.

Jason Gonzales lives with his partner and two children in the big trees and wildness of Oregon's Coast Range. Recently, their family's activism is geared to forest defense, and creating multi-generational spaces and family supportive behaviors in the various fights to save the ancient giants of the Pacific Northwest.

Tiny (a.k.a. Lisa Gray-Garcia) is a poverty scholar, revolutionary journalist, lecturer, Indigenous Taino, Roma mama of Tiburcio, daughter of Dee, and the cofounder of POOR Magazine. She is also the author of *Criminal of Poverty: Growing Up Homeless in America.* Her newest book to be released in 2012 is titled *Poverty Scholarship: a PeopleSteXt—the Population Brings the Popular Education.*

Jessica Hoffmann is a coeditor/copublisher of *make/shift magazine* and auntie of the marvelous Ruby Joy Hoffmann.

Heather Jackson is a survivor, a bisexual leftist radical feminist vegan Occupy activist, and a sober single mom to an intelligent and funny ten-year-old vegetarian girl. She works as a doula and bikes everywhere. She will be finishing a Masters degree in counseling and women studies in May 2012.

Rahula Janowski is an anarchist mama from a white working class background. She is a facilitator, mediator, kitchen witch, and pink collar worker. She's an avid consumer of dystopian speculative fiction who is still hoping for and working for a utopian future and collective liberation.

Sine Hwang Jensen is an Asian descendant caregiver, organizer, and musician from Baltimore. Her work centers on racial justice, anti-oppression education, healing, and restoring dignity.

Agnes Johnson was born in Brooklyn, NY. She is a graduate of the High School of Performing Arts and attended SUNY at Farmingdale and Buffalo. She has danced, taught, and been an advocate for the arts throughout the United States and now once again lives in New York. She has one daughter, Mia, who is her jewel and gift to the world.

Simon Knaphus likes homegrown tomatoes, reading, his two kids, and making vegan food. He is a tranny papa living in the Pacific Northwest.

Victoria Law (co-editor) is a mother, photographer, and writer. She is the author of *Resistance Behind Bars: The Struggles of Incarcerated Women*, which won the 2009 PASS (Prevention for a Safer Society) Award and earned her the 2011 Brooklyn College Young Alumna Award.

Carina Lomeli is a San Francisco Bay Area based political activist, impressionist Xicana artist, and daughter of migrants from Santiago Tangamandapio, Michoacán. Since 2008, she has been teaching and learning at POOR Magazine, where her revolutionary work includes translation, visionary art, and documentation through all forms of media including radio, film, and organizing. You can learn more at http://www.carinalomeli.com.

London Pro-Feminist Men's Group was a group of men who met in London every two weeks from 2007 to 2010. They engaged in a combination of consciousness-raising and activism. The aims of their meetings were to support each other in their personal struggles as men, including their efforts to rid themselves of sexist behavior; to discuss issues around gender politics generally; and to plan and co-ordinate pro-feminist actions.

Amariah Love is a queer sparkly radical childcare activist residing in her beloved community in Atlanta, Georgia. She graduated from Georgia State University with a BA in Sociology and Women's Studies, makes her living being a nanny, and passionately organizes with Kelli's Childcare Collective of Atlanta, an organization she founded in June 2010 in honor of her late mother Kelli.

Monalisa Lennon Diallo, a.k.a. Oluko Lumumba, is a deep thinker and compassionate soul who creates everyday revolution with each breath and stroke of the keyboard. She is a radical mother of three mostly grown children: Jewel, Paul, Dyson; a mother-in-law to Naw; and a grandmother to Ala, all of whom are her heart's inspiration. She is also a teacher by calling.

mama racoon is a single mom who lives with her ten-year-old daughter in the Midwest. She loves animals, the fall, and nice people, and has been a part of free food, anti-globalization, and Latin American solidarity movements.

Mamas of Color Rising and Young Women United are both local affiliates of INCITE! Women of Color Against Violence, a national activist organization of radical feminists of color advancing a movement to end violence against women of color and their communities through direct action, critical dialogue, and grassroots organizing.

Widely known as the grandma of the mama zine scene and a pioneer in the genre of radical parenting writing, *China Martens* (co-editor) raised her daughter as a single mother on welfare and working poor while continuing to put out *The Future Generation,* the longest-running parenting zine in the history of the Western world (1990 to the present). Her daughter is nearly twenty-four years old and her zine has been anthologized into the book *The Future Generation: The Zine-Book for Subculture Parents, Kids, Friends and Others* (Atomic Book Company, 2007).

Noemi Martinez lives in the texas/mexico borderlands of the Rio Grande Valley, birthplace of Gloria Anzaldua. A single mami writer/poet and spiller of secrets living in occupied land, her latest adventures and unicorn sightings can be read at www.hermanaresist.com.

Kathleen McIntyre, LMSW, lives in Queens and is interested in exploring the ways we can help each other heal from loss and trauma as a way to strengthen our alternative communities. She edits *The Worst* zine on grief and loss, and for fun and survival, she is a member of the For the Birds feminist collective. Please send zine submissions and silly cat pictures to: theworstzine@gmail.com.

Stacey "cripchick" Milbern is a disability justice activist, blogger, and youth worker living in the Bay Area.

Jessica Mills is a rock star, mom, and author of the book *My Mother Wears Combat Boots: A Parenting Guide for the Rest of Us*. She has been involved in community projects across the country and is currently part of the local food revolution in Albuquerque, New Mexico, where she lives with her partner Ernesto and two daughters, Emma-Joy and Maya-Rae.

Tomas Moniz is the founder, editor, and a writer for the award-winning zine *Rad Dad*. Looking for radical parenting community, he created *Rad Dad* to provide the space for parents (and in particular fathers) to share, commiserate, plan, and support each other in challenging patriarchy one diaper at a time. He is helping to raise three children and lives with a menagerie of animals in Berkeley, California.

Coleen Murphy lives, reads, writes, takes pictures, makes zines, and infrequently blogs from New Orleans, where she lives with her two unschooled sons. Her work has been published in *HipMama, Fertile Ground, MamaPhiles* and *Breeder*. She publishes the Mama Calendar annually, and *Once Upon a Photobooth* every so often.

Maegan "la Mamita Mala" Ortiz is a badass radical Rican mami media maker/blogger writer/poeta/performer, independent journalist, and the original twitterputa.

Encian Pastel has played and organized with the Bay Area Childcare Collective since 2008. He is inspired by the creative inventiveness of children and seeks to channel their power when developing resources for adults.

Traci Picard is an herbalist who operates an apothecary in Providence where she makes, sells, and barters herbal medicine and teaches people about herbs. She writes about plants, holistic health care, and life while homeschooling her three children.

Amanda Rich is a community organizer, farmer, and poet living in Albuquerque, New Mexico, with her partner, April, and their dog, goats, and chickens. A radical both at heart and in the practical sense, she's been a conscientious ally to parents and kids in her community, even prior to becoming a caretaker herself.

Fabiola Sandoval lives, works, and plays in Los Angeles with her daughter Amaya, who also writes.

Cynthia Ann Schemmer is a writer who recently moved to Philadelphia after not leaving New York for twenty-eight years. She writes and produces the oral history print and audio zine *Habits of Being* and has been published in *Connotation Press* and *RE/VISIONIST*. She is a member of For the Birds feminist collective and is biding her time until she can own many gigantic dogs.

Mikaela Shafer lives in a colorful cave with her best friend Bryan, their ghost baby Paikea, and their amazing miracle babe Hunter.

Kate Shapiro lives and loves in the South. Currently living and working in Western North Carolina with the Center for Participatory Change, she is happiest when she is supporting youth organizing, farming, cooking, and playing games. She is a member of Song and Project South and sits on the Vision and Strategies Council for Kindred, a Southern healing justice collective.

Mustafa Shukur is an existentialist, a cultural Muslim, an anti-theist, a social anarchist, a father, loved partner, and a poet.

Jennifer Silverman is a NYC-based mama of two sons and an unrepentant coffee addict. She is a co-editor of *My Baby Rides the Short Bus* (PM Press, 2009) and has had essays and articles published in *HipMama* magazine, *Newsday*, *off our backs*, and many regional newspapers and parenting magazines. Jennifer has also spoken about raising her son with autism, intergenerational movement-building, and community organized childcare at conferences including the Left Forum, National Conference on Organized Resistance, Mama Gathering, and several bookfairs, and is looking forward to the day when there is less talk and more action on these issues.

Born at home in Baltimore, *Harriet Moon Smith* is a kitten-loving queer womyn radical, committed to feminism and racial justice. In addition to organizing with Kidz City, Harriet is a former substitute teacher and current auntie. Her education and paid work has centered on wellness and health care, and she is the self-appointed first-aid mistress in Kidz City.

Poet, writer, educator *Mariahadessa Ekere Tallie* is a mother of two daughters and a student of herbal medicine. Her first book of poetry, *Karma's Footsteps*, was released in Fall 2011. Her booklet, *Mother Nature: Thoughts on Nourishing your Body, Mind, and Spirit During Pregnancy and Beyond* is available free online at www.ekeretallie.com.

Before becoming a Director of Development for nonprofits promoting education and social justice, *Darran White Tilghman* was a professional pastry baker. She lives in Baltimore with her husband Ben, their daughter Susannah, and their cat Lou.

Jessica Trimbath, otherwise known as *Davka*, lives, writes, and designs jewelry in Ojai, California. Her work has been featured in *make/shift magazine*, *Weave Magazine*, *The New Yinzer*, and *$pread*.

Maxina Ventura is a longtime anarchist activist who chose not to send her kids to any school. They are great learners and pretty wonderful people, helping most recently to set up the Occupy Berkeley encampment in the SF Bay Area. Max is a singer grown on bluegrass and old-time music, and trained in the classical musical world. For many years, she has been exposing the folly of activist movements trying to separate parents and kids.

Mari Villaluna, a POOR Magazine indigenous scholar and Indigenous Peoples Media Project Coordinator, has just recently relocated from a reservation in the Southwest back to her birthplace of San Francisco. She is committed to standing as the source of transformation for our people's healing and being that source of love even when people don't even love themselves. She is a cofounder of the Eagle and Condor Healing Project, which aims to support family reunification and birth in Indigenous communities by providing healing spaces, performance art, and one-on-one consulting with individuals and organizations.

Acknowledgments

Victoria's Acknowledgments:

Without the ongoing support from friends, family, and community, neither raising my daughter Siu Loong nor creating this book would have been possible. There are so many people to thank over the course of my nearly twelve years of parenting (and the past six years of building *Don't Leave Your Friends Behind*) that I would have to create a whole new zine to include them all. Just know, each and every one of you, that, without you, the life I have would not have been possible. Thank you.

China's Acknowledgments:

This book is dedicated to all who struggle: you are not alone. I want to acknowledge the pain and difficulty and seriousness of why this book was made. The stories that are not in this book, but behind why this book was made. Our goal was to create a positive resource but not to make you feel like a failure if you don't have these resources. This is not an easy topic! It is quite difficult to work on. I want to acknowledge that difficulty.

Special thanks to my mom and dad for all their support, and to Steve Saunders (Lucy and DV's dad) for putting in a new hot water heater for free while I worked on the manuscript. Also to Lucy N. Morris and Wren Cooke for sharing my excitement about reading and writing during our tutoring class. And to Sara Morris for all the vegetables and eggs from the farm. With love always to my daughter Nadja Martens, my cousins Jane Williamson and Michelle North, and my nieces Jade and Lara Martens.

These are indisputably momentous times – the financial system is melting down globally and the Empire is stumbling. Now more than ever there is a vital need for radical ideas.

In the four years since its founding—and on a mere shoestring—PM Press has risen to the formidable challenge of publishing and distributing knowledge and entertainment for the struggles ahead. With over 175 releases to date, we have published an impressive and stimulating array of literature, art, music, politics, and culture. Using every available medium, we've succeeded in connecting those hungry for ideas and information to those putting them into practice.

Friends of PM allows you to directly help impact, amplify, and revitalize the discourse and actions of radical writers, filmmakers, and artists. It provides us with a stable foundation from which we can build upon our early successes and provides a much-needed subsidy for the materials that can't necessarily pay their own way. You can help make that happen —and receive every new title automatically delivered to your door once a month—by joining as a Friend of PM Press. And, we'll throw in a free T-Shirt when you sign up.

Here are your options:
- $25 a month: Get all books and pamphlets plus 50% discount on all webstore purchases
- $40 a month: Get all PM Press releases (including CDs and DVDs) plus 50% discount on all webstore purchases
- $100 a month: Superstar—Everything plus PM merchandise, free downloads, and 50% discount on all webstore purchases

For those who can't afford $25 or more a month, we're introducing Sustainer Rates at $15, $10 and $5. Sustainers get a free PM Press t-shirt and a 50% discount on all purchases from our website.

Your Visa or Mastercard will be billed once a month, until you tell us to stop. Or until our efforts succeed in bringing the revolution around. Or the financial meltdown of Capital makes plastic redundant. Whichever comes first.

PM Press was founded at the end of 2007 by a small collection of folks with decades of publishing, media, and organizing experience. PM Press co-conspirators have published and distributed hundreds of books, pamphlets, CDs, and DVDs. Members of PM have founded enduring book fairs, spearheaded victorious tenant organizing campaigns, and worked closely with bookstores, academic conferences, and even rock bands to deliver political and challenging ideas to all walks of life. We're old enough to know what we're doing and young enough to know what's at stake.

We seek to create radical and stimulating fiction and non-fiction books, pamphlets, t-shirts, visual and audio materials to entertain, educate and inspire you. We aim to distribute these through every available channel with every available technology—whether that means you are seeing anarchist classics at our bookfair stalls; reading our latest vegan cookbook at the café; downloading geeky fiction e-books; or digging new music and timely videos from our website.

PM Press is always on the lookout for talented and skilled volunteers, artists, activists and writers to work with. If you have a great idea for a project or can contribute in some way, please get in touch.

PM Press
PO Box 23912
Oakland CA 94623
510-658-3906
www.pmpress.org

ALSO AVAILABLE FROM PM PRESS

Resistance Behind Bars: The Struggles Of Incarcerated Women, 2nd Edition
by Victoria Law
ISBN: 978-1-60486-583-7
$20.00

In 1974, women imprisoned at New York's maximum-security prison at Bedford Hills staged what is known as the August Rebellion. Protesting the brutal beating of a fellow prisoner, the women fought off guards, holding seven of them hostage, and took over sections of the prison.

While many have heard of the 1971 Attica prison uprising, the August Rebellion remains relatively unknown even in activist circles. *Resistance Behind Bars* is determined to challenge and change such oversights. As it examines daily struggles against appalling prison conditions and injustices, Resistance documents both collective organizing and individual resistance among women incarcerated in the U.S. Emphasizing women's agency in resisting the conditions of their confinement through forming peer education groups, clandestinely arranging ways for children to visit mothers in distant prisons and raising public awareness about their lives, Resistance seeks to spark further discussion and research into the lives of incarcerated women and galvanize much-needed outside support for their struggles.

This updated and revised edition of the 2009 PASS Award winning book includes a new chapter about transgender, transsexual, intersex, and gender-variant people in prison.

Praise:

"Victoria Law's eight years of research and writing, inspired by her unflinching commitment to listen to and support women prisoners, has resulted in an illuminating effort to document the dynamic resistance of incarcerated women in the United States." —Roxanne Dunbar-Ortiz

"Written in regular English, rather than academese, this is an impressive work of research and reportage" —Mumia Abu-Jamal, death row political prisoner and author of *Live From Death Row*

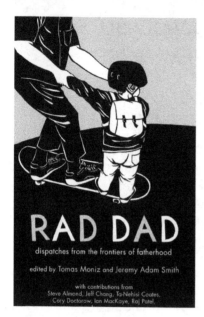

ALSO AVAILABLE FROM PM PRESS

The unabashedly human experience of raising kids with disabilities

edited by Yantra Bertelli, Jennifer Silverman and Sarah Talbot

My Baby Rides the Short Bus: The Unabashedly Human Experience of Raising Kids with Disabilities
Edited by Yantra Bertelli, Jennifer Silverman, and Sarah Talbot
ISBN: 978-1-60486-109-9
$20.00

In lives where there is a new diagnosis or drama every day, the stories in this collection provide parents of "special needs" kids with a welcome chuckle, a rock to stand on, and a moment of reality held far enough from the heart to see clearly. Featuring works by "alternative" parents who have attempted to move away from mainstream thought--or remove its influence altogether--this anthology, taken as a whole, carefully considers the implications of parenting while raising children with disabilities.

From professional writers to novice storytellers including Robert Rummel-Hudson, Ayun Halliday, and Kerry Cohen, this assortment of authentic, shared experiences from parents at the fringe of the fringes is a partial antidote to the stories that misrepresent, ridicule, and objectify disabled kids and their parents.

Praise:

"This is a collection of beautifully written stories, incredibly open and well articulated, complicated and diverse: about human rights and human emotions. About love, and difficulties; informative and supportive. Wise, non-conformist, and absolutely punk rock!" —China Martens, author of *The Future Generation: The Zine-Book for Subculture Parents, Kids, Friends and Others*

"If only that lady in the grocery store and all of those other so-called parenting experts would read this book! These true-life tales by mothers and fathers raising kids with 'special needs' on the outer fringes of mainstream America are by turns empowering, heartbreaking, inspiring, maddening, and even humorous. Readers will be moved by the bold honesty of these voices, and by the fierce love and determination that rings throughout. This book is a vital addition to the public discourse on disability." —Suzanne Kamata, editor of *Love You to Pieces: Creative Writers on Raising a Child with Special Needs*

ALSO AVAILABLE FROM PM PRESS

Sometimes the Spoon Runs Away with Another Spoon Coloring Book
by Jacinta Bunnell
and Nathaniel Kusinitz
ISBN: 978-1-60486-329-1
$10.00

We have the power to change fairy tales and nursery rhymes so that these stories are more realistic. In *Sometimes the Spoon Runs Away With Another Spoon* you will find anecdotes of real kids' lives and true-to-life fairy tale characters. This book pushes us beyond rigid gender expectations while we color fantastic beasts who like pretty jewelry and princesses who build rocket ships.

Celebrate sensitive boys, tough girls, and others who do not fit into a disempowering gender categorization.

Sometimes the Spoon. . . aids the work of dismantling the Princess Industrial Complex by moving us forward with more honest representations of our children and ourselves. Color to your heart's content. Laugh along with the characters. Write your own fairy tales. Share your own truths.

Praise:

"As moving and funny as *Walter the Farting Dog*, with pictures you can color however your heart desires, *Sometimes the Spoon. . .* is appropriate for children of all ages, especially those who grew up without it." —Ayun Halliday, Chief Primatologist of *The East Village Inky*

"For some people the sky's the limit. For Jacinta Bunnell it's a place to put a rainbow. There are no limits in *Sometimes the Spoon Runs Away With Another Spoon*— just fun and love. Jacinta Bunnell invites you to "Step right up!" to the wonderful world of you!" —World Famous *BOB*, *Ultimate Self Confidence! Coach*

ALSO AVAILABLE FROM PM PRESS

Organize!: Building from the Local for Global Justice
Edited by Aziz Choudry, Jill Hanley,
and Eric Shragge
ISBN: 978-1-60486-433-5
$24.95

What are the ways forward for organizing for progressive social change in an era of unprecedented economic, social, and ecological crises? How do political activists build power and critical analysis in their daily work for change?

Grounded in struggles in Canada, the United States, Aotearoa/New Zealand, as well as transnational activist networks, *Organize!: Building from the Local for Global Justice* links local organizing with global struggles to make a better world. In over twenty chapters written by a diverse range of organizers, activists, academics, lawyers, artists, and researchers, this book weaves a rich and varied tapestry of dynamic strategies for struggle. From community-based labor organizing strategies among immigrant workers to mobilizing psychiatric survivors, from arts and activism for Palestine to organizing in support of Indigenous Peoples, the authors reflect critically on the tensions, problems, limits, and gains inherent in a diverse range of organizing contexts and practices. The book also places these processes in historical perspective, encouraging us to use history to shed light on contemporary injustices and how they can be overcome. Written in accessible language, *Organize!* will appeal to college and university students, activists, organizers and the wider public.

Contributors include: Aziz Choudry, Jill Hanley, Eric Shragge, Devlin Kuyek, Kezia Speirs, Evelyn Calugay, Anne Petermann, Alex Law, Jared Will, Radha D'Souza, Edward Ou Jin Lee, Norman Nawrocki, Rafeef Ziadah, Maria Bargh, Dave Bleakney, Abdi Hagi Yusef, Mostafa Henaway, Emilie Breton, Sandra Jeppesen, Anna Kruzynski, Rachel Sarrasin, Dolores Chew, David Reville, Kathryn Church, Brian Aboud, Joey Calugay, Gada Mahrouse, Harsha Walia, Mary Foster, Martha Stiegman, Robert Fisher, Yuseph Katiya, and Christopher Reid.

ALSO AVAILABLE FROM PM PRESS

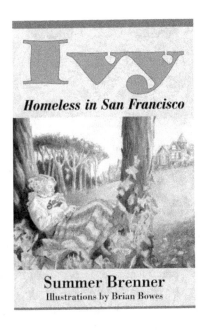

Ivy, Homeless in San Francisco
by Summer Brenner
ISBN: 978-1-60486-317-8
$15.00

In this empathetic tale of hope, understanding, and the importance of family, young readers confront the difficult issues of poverty and the hardships of homelessness. Its inspiring young heroine is Ivy, who finds herself homeless on the streets of San Francisco when she and her father, Poppy, are evicted from their artist loft.

Struggling to survive day to day, Ivy and Poppy befriend a dog who leads them to the ramshackle home of octogenarian siblings, Eugenia and Oscar Orr. This marks the start of a series of desperate and joyful adventures that blend a spoonful of Charles Dickens's *Oliver Twist* with a dash of Armistead Maupin's *Tales of the City* and a few pinches of the *Adventures of Lassie*. Ivy's tale will appeal to young readers and adults, providing much material for discussion between generations.

Praise:

Recipient of the Children's Literary Classics and MOONBEAM awards

"*Ivy* is an engaging, educational experience, with emotional range, density of characters, a cinematic visual imagination, and a heroine wild at heart. We have a lot to learn about homelessness, and Summer Brenner's saga of fractured family and redeeming friendship takes us deep inside the experience, while agitating our broader concern with social justice. All this in a lucid, poetic prose. She not only will get young people to read but make them want to write as well." —John Broughton, associate professor of psychology & education, Teachers College, Columbia University

"...Lolitas, Oliver Twists, and Huckleberry Finns live on, and now, Ivy's tale of hope lives right alongside them." —Robin Clewley, *San Francisco Chronicle*

ANARCHIST PEDAGOGIES

COLLECTIVE ACTIONS, THEORIES,
AND CRITICAL REFLECTIONS ON EDUCATION

ALSO AVAILABLE FROM PM PRESS

Anarchist Pedagogies:
Collective Actions, Theories, and
Critical Reflections on Education
Edited by Robert H. Haworth
ISBN: 978-1-60486-484-7
$24.95

Education is a challenging subject for anarchists. Many are critical about working within a state-run education system that is embedded in hierarchical, standardized, and authoritarian structures. Numerous individuals and collectives envision the creation of counterpublics or alternative educational sites as possible forms of resistance, while other anarchists see themselves as "saboteurs" within the public arena—believing that there is a need to contest dominant forms of power and educational practices from multiple fronts. Of course, if anarchists agree that there are no blueprints for education, the question remains, in what dynamic and creative ways can we construct nonhierarchical, anti-authoritarian, mutual, and voluntary educational spaces?

Contributors to this edited volume engage readers in important and challenging issues in the area of anarchism and education. From Francisco Ferrer's modern schools in Spain and the Work People's College in the United States, to contemporary actions in developing "free skools" in the U.K. and Canada, to direct-action education such as learning to work as a "street medic" in the protests against neoliberalism, the contributors illustrate the importance of developing complex connections between educational theories and collective actions. Anarchists, activists, and critical educators should take these educational experiences seriously as they offer invaluable examples for potential teaching and learning environments outside of authoritarian and capitalist structures. Major themes in the volume include: learning from historical anarchist experiments in education, ways that contemporary anarchists create dynamic and situated learning spaces, and finally, critically reflecting on theoretical frameworks and educational practices.

Contributors include: David Gabbard, Jeffery Shantz, Isabelle Fremeaux & John Jordan, Abraham P. DeLeon, Elsa Noterman, Andre Pusey, Matthew Weinstein, Alex Khasnabish, and many others.

ALSO AVAILABLE FROM PM PRESS

*Anarchism and Education:
A Philosophical Perspective*
by Judith Suissa
ISBN: 978-1-60486-114-3
$19.95

While there have been historical accounts of the anarchist school movement, there has been no systematic work on the philosophical underpinnings of anarchist educational ideas—until now.

Anarchism and Education offers a philosophical account of the neglected tradition of anarchist thought on education. Although few anarchist thinkers wrote systematically on education, this analysis is based largely on a reconstruction of the educational thought of anarchist thinkers gleaned from their various ethical, philosophical and popular writings. Primarily drawing on the work of the nineteenth century anarchist theorists such as Bakunin, Kropotkin and Proudhon, the book also covers twentieth century anarchist thinkers such as Noam Chomsky, Paul Goodman, Daniel Guerin and Colin Ward.

This original work will interest philosophers of education and educationalist thinkers as well as those with a general interest in anarchism.

Praise:

"This is an excellent book that deals with important issues through the lens of anarchist theories and practices of education. . . The book tackles a number of issues that are relevant to anybody who is trying to come to terms with the philosophy of education." —*Higher Education Review*

ALSO AVAILABLE FROM PM PRESS

The Real Cost Of Prisons Comix
Edited by Lois Ahrens
ISBN: 978-1-60486-034-4
$14.95

Winner of the 2008 PASS Award (Prevention for a Safer Society) from the National Council on Crime and Delinquency

One out of every hundred adults in the U.S. is in prison. This book provides a crash course in what drives mass incarceration, the human and community costs, and how to stop the numbers from going even higher. This volume collects the three comic books published by the Real Cost of Prisons Project. The stories and statistical information in each comic book is thoroughly researched and documented.

Prison Town: Paying the Price tells the story of how the financing and site locations of prisons affects the people of rural communities in which prison are built. It also tells the story of how mass incarceration affects people of urban communities where the majority of incarcerated people come from.

Prisoners of the War on Drugs includes the history of the war on drugs, mandatory minimums, how racism creates harsher sentences for people of color, stories on how the war on drugs works against women, three strikes laws, obstacles to coming home after incarceration, and how mass incarceration destabilizes neighborhoods.

Prisoners of a Hard Life: Women and Their Children includes stories about women trapped by mandatory sentencing and the "costs" of incarceration for women and their families. Also included are alternatives to the present system, a glossary, and footnotes.

Over 125,000 copies of the comic books have been printed and more than 100,000 have been sent to families of people who are incarcerated, people who are incarcerated, and to organizers and activists throughout the country. The book includes a chapter with descriptions about how the comix have been put to use in the work of organizers and activists in prison and in the "free world" by ESL teachers, high school teachers, college professors, students, and health care providers throughout the country. The demand for them is constant and the ways in which they are being used is inspiring.